Lázaro Francisco Acosta Ruiz

Near death experience

AF154055

Lázaro Francisco Acosta Ruiz

Near death experience

and other phenomena of the mindfrom the
perspective of Mechanics
QuantumEpistemological View

JustFiction Edition

Imprint

Any brand names and product names mentioned in this book are subject to trademark, brand or patent protection and are trademarks or registered trademarks of their respective holders. The use of brand names, product names, common names, trade names, product descriptions etc. even without a particular marking in this work is in no way to be construed to mean that such names may be regarded as unrestricted in respect of trademark and brand protection legislation and could thus be used by anyone.

Cover image: www.ingimage.com

Publisher:
JustFiction! Edition
is a trademark of
Dodo Books Indian Ocean Ltd. and OmniScriptum S.R.L publishing group

120 High Road, East Finchley, London, N2 9ED, United Kingdom
Str. Armeneasca 28/1, office 1, Chisinau MD-2012, Republic of Moldova, Europe
Printed at: see last page
ISBN: 978-620-0-10415-1

Copyright © Lázaro Francisco Acosta Ruiz
Copyright © 2024 Dodo Books Indian Ocean Ltd. and OmniScriptum S.R.L publishing group

Contenido

A CLARIFICATION ABOUT THE ENGLISH VERSION

The first version of this work, published in Spanish, was released in 2023, and a year later, given the low level of sales, the authors decided to upload the work to a free download site, with the purpose of facilitate access to any level of readers. But not just any place, but one where the average reader was a university student: professors, graduates, engineers, and of course, people of letters, regardless of their base specialty.

After a few months, among the chosen portals, one stood out due to the level of downloads made: www.researchgate.net. After a few weeks, the number of downloads made was appreciable, for a work without any endorsement in its favor, but 6 months later, the level of downloads already exceeds the figure of 4000, and everything indicates that it will continue to grow.

The question we immediately asked ourselves was what the result would be today, if the work were also offered, at least, in the English language, which in the case at hand, will not lack the specific interest of thousands of readers. , within the academic field. And that is why we have made this special version, in English.

It is worth highlighting that the expectations are not unfounded: The academic world is not the conducive framework to promote a work focused on topics such as "Near Death Experiences" (NDE), and within that context, seek links with Reincarnation and other spiritualist, parapsychological themes, etc. But at the same time, it is, because within the academic context, the interest of a basically unaware public begins to awaken, but has realized what it needs to know, and a work that goes to the specifics of the issue is very useful, leaving the way open for restless readers, lovers of academia, who satisfy their curiosity in these complicated subjects, whether or not they later want to continue further, in a study in accordance with their cultural and professional interests.

This is the point, and this is the work. If we are right, and our forecasts come true, we will be very satisfied.

El autor

INTRODUCTION

In 2022, when we were already beginning to emerge from the pandemic, the author published the book "HALLUCINATIONS. Poetry beyond death", which is at the same time an exploration into the world of "parapoetry," which includes more than 50 poems, which, to a large extent, are created in the context of parapsychological phenomena. The present work turns out to be a second part of that one, but greatly expanded in all analyzable senses.

And here we must clarify that we are not using the term parapoetry, in the sense that critics use to name a new poetry of these times, which is fundamentally developing on social networks, developed especially by young people who post their poems on YouTube, accompanied of music, images, etc.; and this trend is taking on such magnitude that it is being valued as a new way of doing poetry.

In our case, we associate the term parapoetry, reserved for that poetry that moves within the context of parapsychological or paranormal phenomena, and therefore within a field in principle not accepted at an academic level, which is a matter unrelated to poetic creation, free of ties. But it is still a factor that at a given moment the poet wants to consider, if this determines, to some extent, the content of the work. Because it is one thing for the Moon to be used as a poetic image, and another thing for the Moon to not exist.

Therefore, Hallucinations constituted a first step on the path of trying to establish a "*theoretical*" support, visualizing those situations where phenomena such as Near Death Experiences (NDE) begin to be seen as a reality object of study for Science, This brings it closer to Literature, since talking about "the afterlife" becomes a real fact and not a poetic license or an object within a Science Fiction story.

But also, in this work we intend to use death with a somewhat absurd vision, since it is a death that participates as another character, that moves from one poem to another, but not with the gloomy image that always accompanies it. , but quite the opposite: fighting to save the life of a suicide; or saving the life of an entertained person, who is about to be the victim of an accident, - who knows why the pandemic concerns - and in such circumstances the possibilities of creation are expanded.

We can say then that this work delves into the phenomena of the afterlife, starting with **"Near Death Experiences"**, Reincarnation and other paranormal themes, and we do so for two main reasons: to help the reader who is be interested in the poems included in the last part of the work; and also, summarize the most general ideas of themes – most of them considered "taboo" – widely discussed by authors who pursue diverse purposes, unrelated to poetry, and therefore their contents go deeper, opening a path between the complicated situations that are present in the "*darkness*" of the world of studies of paranormal phenomena, among which numerous medical professionals are already beginning to appear. Therefore, those close to **Psychiatry**, **Hypnosis**, **Psychology**, etc. are qualified within the parapsychological context.

But to all of the above, a combination of scientists who deal with Quantum Physics, and at the same time research in Neuroscience, has been added with great force, which is subdivided into various independent branches, making a "mixed whole" in which they participate. scientific, religious and even literary interests, which have in common a very complicated object of study: the human brain.

That is the panorama that the main author finds, as another scholar, to the extent that his interest, essentially scientific, has increased in the study of the phenomena of the mind, which can no longer be centralized only in the knowledge of **Experiences. Near Death** (NDE), as he initially thought, in the days when he was working on the play "*Hallucinations*".

However, when the decision was made to work from the authorship (and not by professional translators) on a version translated into English, it became clear that it would not make sense to include in it the set of poems included in the original version, in Spanish, because In translation, a good part of the spiritual content is lost, and the meter that in some poems plays a non-literary meaning, and therefore, is not translatable.

Such modification means that this English version is fundamentally dedicated to informing any reader - unrelated to scientific, paranormal knowledge, religious beliefs, etc. –. about current scientific events at a basic level, related to brain phenomena, both neurological and parapsychological; and leaving for the complementary annex, only a few illustrative poems, but in their two versions, that is, in Spanish and the most appropriate translation, into English.

We hope that with this approach, an English-language reader, interested in these topics, will be able to take greater advantage of the work, with the additional benefit that it will be possible to dedicate additional space to consider with greater rigor, author-mediums such as **Allan Kardec** and **Edgar Cayce**, without a doubt the most relevant for the immense work carried out, literary and human, precisely in the English language, regardless of his many multilingual translations, especially related to the various spiritualist currents, in terms of the approach and significance of the reincarnationist currents.

In this sense, the author proposes to make a summary or general account of the different aspects related to life after life, as well defined by **RAYMOND A. MOODY**, one of the first authors who dedicated a large part of his life to doing science. in a context full of misunderstandings and professional ignorance. PhD in philosophy and medicine, in addition to being a psychiatrist, Moody was the first doctor to systematically study the phenomena of survival after bodily death, publishing the result of his research in the **work LIFE AFTER LIFE**.

In this account, which covers themes that deserve to be known as related elements, and not as separate phenomena, we propose to help readers interested in the phenomena of the human mind; and also – why not – readers interested in poetry, because in the unknowns that such phenomena generate, they could find new sources of inspiration to create literature.

There is also a background influence, related to the historical division that Descartes created, when he divided reality into mind (area of religion) and matter (area of science), which we can express in the best way if we quote the Goswami couple, A. (2012), when they state that "*Fortunately (...) **quantum physics** has created a window for the integration of science and spirituality..*" That is the starting point.

As authors, we consider that, due to its structure and combination of contents, this work is truly unique, and we hope that the English-language reader, possibly more poet than scientist, will not mind excusing the remaining gaps related to the diverse content. Therefore, it is advisable to make it clear from the beginning, to those potential readers who wish to consult in depth the various contents discussed here, that this is not the work they need. In that sense, there are plenty of well-known titles and authors on the shelves of bookstores and libraries in English-speaking countries.

CHAPTER I

Everything mixe...

1.1   For a science without limits

We are at a time when paranormal phenomena are awakening an unusual interest, not only among the common citizen, but also among personalities from the most different professions, and first of all, **Medical Sciences**, with research on the brain at the forefront: and **Theoretical Physics** very closely, after the spectacular discoveries and confirmations produced in **Quantum Mechanics**, which allow a radically different approach to the study not only of the brain, but also of the **Biology**, **Biochemistry** and **Genetics** associated with it, to the point that there are hypotheses that attempt to demonstrate that it is not Genetics that decides what we are and will be (as biological beings, and that determines or models our consciousness) but that the opposite is true: our mind, which is definitely modeled energy (for who we are) to the point of being able to modify our own DNA, transmittable to our offspring (Lipton, B, 2007).

Could there be a relationship between Near Death Experiences (NDEs), Reincarnation, Quantum Physics, certain paranormal phenomena (Carter, C. 2010; Greyson, B. 2014) and even Ufology, which studies the mysteries of life alien? (Benítez, J.J, 2023)

In this work we are going to explore a hypothesis that could connect some of the most fascinating and mysterious topics in science and spirituality. It is about the possibility of considering that Near Death Experiences (NDEs), Reincarnation, Quantum Physics, the research of **Jacobo Grinberg**, paranormal phenomena and extraterrestrials, have some type of relationship with each other. Technically a mixed whole, full of questions to be resolved, which has motivated authors like Amit Goswami for decades.

But attention: the main objective of the work is to leave these possibilities open to creation, not only from a context considered paranormal, but from knowledge supported, as far as possible, by established science, considering that it could be a source of inspiration. for writers and poets, especially the latter. Because in these times, the "*beyond*" is increasingly "here", closer to a reality that makes it immensely more poetic.

Certainly in the last 20 years everything has been written and published, and in the modest opinion of the authors, who are not experts in any of the subjects under study, the result tips the balance in favor of a "YES" , which is above all a vote for Science, in the certainty that sooner rather than later its world will be enriched, expanding the poetic vision of the mysteries being investigated.

But it must also be said that not all knowledge comes from unaccredited sources, although even the most respectable specialists who today investigate these topics have not openly received the favor of the Academies. There is, however, a point of commonality between all these branches and authors, which have generally been explored separately, and that is that in one way or another, they are all related to the **HUMAN BRAIN**.

It must be said that the advances made in brain research in recent decades have generalized a global interest in the development of Neurosciences, only that this development goes in a direction, solidly supported by scientific research in Medicine, Biology, Physics and a broad set of fully established and automated sciences, backed by Nobel Prizes and other recognitions, which studies on NDEs do not have, just to mention the path of the paranormal. In short, the study of the brain is a common element, with more unknowns than results.

We could argue, however, that better perspectives did not support Faraday, when faced with a questioning question from the academics of his time (Cadavid, A. 2004), asking him "what is the use of that electricity" that he showed them, Faraday responded to his once with a question, which demonstrates his extraordinary vision of the future:

"And what is the use of a newly born child?"

But just as Faraday perceived that he was not walking on wrong ground, within those common elements that have been explored almost blindly, there is one that definitively opens the doors to an epistemological environment capable of conceptually changing many things, and that object of study is: **Quantum Mechanics...**

1.2 The epistemological barrier Who imposes the limits?

Due to the knowledge that has been accumulated over the course of centuries, having as its main weapon certain mathematical devices that operate with respect to a certain Wave Function, which in common language would be equivalent to fighting with the help of ghosts.

Fig. 1. Does Science have limits?

But since what we intend in this long familiarization is to leave open the problem that gives numinous meaning to the contents, which in turn open a space different from the poetics that the book deals with, we will limit ourselves to presenting, with the help of the diagram shown , the epistemological model that allows us to better understand the formal limits of science today.

This plate, in itself, is an allegory of human knowledge, and is taken from an introductory lecture on the concept of Science, given by the author to professors of Medical Sciences. Its hidden objective is to call for reflection on the concept of Science, which authors and teachers sometimes present in an extremely formal way.

In fact, it is far from presenting finished content. It was built live, step by step, in the first part of the class, with the participation of the students, who are not students, since they are also professors of different specialties.

It is simply intended to show that the limits of that formality, which has been delimited over time, only establishes whether or not a discipline is science, considering an imaginary line such that the closer a discipline is to that epistemological barrier. , the more so it will be of the border that separates constituted science, from what is marked in scientific literature with the adjective Pseudoscience. But who or what authority decides on that?

We cannot continue the analysis without first presenting the Concept of Pseudoscience, officially issued by the AMM **Declaration on Pseudosciences and Pseudotherapies in the field of health**, Adopted by the 71st General Assembly of the AMM (online), Córdoba, Spain , October 2020. In accordance with what was expressed in its first section:

> *"Pseudoscience" (false science) is called the set of statements, assumptions, methods, beliefs or practices that, without following a recognized and validated scientific method, are falsely presented as scientific or based on evidence..*

Furthermore, the following question stands out.

> *There is a risk that patients will abandon medical therapies or preventive measures that have been shown to be effective in favor of practices that have not demonstrated curative value, and this can sometimes lead to treatment failure in serious illnesses, which can even lead to death.*

For those interested in consulting the original document, the web address is:

https://www.wma.net/es/policies-post/declaracion-de-la-amm-sobre-pseudociencias-y-pseudoterapias-en-el-campo-de-la-salud/

But we must point out something in this regard. Exactly the same could be said of the patients who lost their health technicians, who attended to the effective treatments they received, with the techniques that in some countries are called physiotherapy and others that, after the aforementioned official statements of the AMM, They were considered in some countries as pseudo therapies, leaving hundreds of technicians who applied them unemployed.

If we return to the diagram in fig. 1, we will see how many disciplines hover around the limit line, among them Pedagogy, because for certain authors Pedagogy does not have a scientifically validable theoretical body, and its object of study mixes tools and techniques, with theoretical elements taken or imported from sciences such as Psychology.

A similar situation occurs with Psychiatry, which for some is a Science - included within Medical Sciences - and for others it is not, especially when talking about techniques such as *Hypnosis*, especially if it includes *Regressions* among its tools, absolutely rejected within the academic context.

We finally have to analyze the case of **Quantum Mechanics**. The scheme presents this discipline cut sharply by the epistemological line of knowledge. But curiously, no one questions this fact, and even less so after the resounding success, with the recent (2022) awarding of the Nobel Prize in Physics, to Quantum Mechanics, in recognition of the research results of physicists Alain Aspect (French), the American John Clauser and the Austrian Anton Zeilinger, when demonstrating the existence of **Quantum Entanglement** (Royal Swedish Academy of Sciences, 2022). We will talk about that in the rest of the work.

In other words: open doors in the afterlife, to lovers of Physics, but also of poetry.

CHAPTER II

Life after life.
Basic count

Generalities

I must first of all clarify – and we are already breaking formalisms and moving on to the first person – that I am not an author very familiar with the already diverse manifestations of so-called paranormal phenomena, and especially those related to Near Death Experiences (NDE). I could say, in any case, that until today I have been an amateur, who is beginning to understand these matters better - and therefore, recognizes them as an Object of Study - and thinks that other people are probably going through a similar situation. In practice, we are ignorant, and a variety of facts that are apparently not interrelated, such as readings, videos, etc., end up creating confusion in the reader, unable for the moment to identify the differences between one phenomenon and another.

On the other hand, for reasons of age, it is not the objective of this interlocutor to achieve full dedication to the study in these fields, but from the beginning we see here new avenues for the development of literature – and not necessarily from Science Fiction, (which has never interested me) but from a dimension open to creativity, where the poet or writer can develop themes based on new realities, much more objective, than a police chase over time, which ends up getting out of control of the pen, and of the patience of a reader who even accepts traveling "to the beyond," but always with his feet in "hereafter."

It is good to clarify that the above is valid for the issue of extraterrestrials and UFO phenomena, which have increased exponentially in recent years, which is logical, due to the development of communication networks, social networks, etc. We are not talking about Science Fiction, we repeat. Within those trends that we previously pointed out, there is a not very widespread one that ensures the existence of extraterrestrial contact "*in the afterlife*", based on quantum theories that enable high energy exchanges, in higher dimensions, starting from the 5th. We will discuss more details about this when we discuss the work of

Jacobo Grinberg, the same one who disappeared without a trace, after his statements about the real possibility of time travel on a mental level, even leaving behind the legend that He is still alive, stuck in the 5th dimension. Each person is the owner of thinking about the existence of other realities, and if they are founded or explainable with theoretical support, so much the better.

For my part, I agree to believe the basic plot of Trojan Horse, the work of J.J. Benítez, and I enjoy it seen as a historical story (others may consider it a novel), and I believe the plot of the vials to the past... So why not leave the door of mysteries open, waiting for the triumphant return of Grinberg , and not precisely from the beyond? I imagine the following headline: Grinberg is alive and works at 5th! dimension!

But I reiterate that we are talking about Science, not Science Fiction. They are obviously different points of view. Talking about Science is not fiction...

For this author, who since he was a child mentally accompanied Verne on many of his trips, and with him he returned from the Moon, and traveled to the Center of the Earth, returning through Stromboli. But it is also perfectly credible to be able to see Jesus crucified, and suffer his passion - even if one does not profess any religion, nor is one atheist without a solution - to the point of even traveling with Grinberg to another dimension... In short, one had to wonder if the work of J.J. Benítez is Science Fiction, because History Fiction it is not. But... And Science? There are plenty of fundamentals...

It is then worth making a summary that allows people interested in the topic to have on hand a general summary that includes the main paranormal phenomena, which have interesting facts; and above all, introduce the reader to the main researchers and specialists who are working to dignify these branches of scientific knowledge – why not say it, if the methods that are applied are – leaving for the end of the work, in the bibliographical references , a list that includes links to books, videos and movies that those interested can access.

2.0 Ten paths in the search for a truth

Although spiritualism integrates many of the aspects that we are going to analyze in these pages, it is not in itself the object of study towards the search for a truth: Is there life after life?

In this work we are going to explore 10 paths that directly allow us to explore the answer to that question.

Without further ado, let's explore the following situations, as an object of study:

1. **Near-death experiences (NDE)**
2. **Reincarnation**
3. **Regressions through hypnosis**
4. **The Medium Unit**
5. **Channeling**
6. **Instrumental Transcommunication**
7. **The Akashic Records**
8. **The research of Scientist Jacobo Grinberg.**
9. **Do donors "speak" through recipients?**
10. **The discoveries of Bruce LIpton**

We will briefly summarize each topic, a difficult task, because there are already books that deal with these aspects in depth, also including multiple examples, without forgetting that hundreds of very well-made videos are the irreplaceable illustration to explain each case. As we already mentioned, the corresponding references are given in the suggested bibliography so that those interested can go directly to those sources.

2.1 Near Death Experiences (NDE)

According to classical sources, the so-called "Near Death Experiences" (NDEs) are psychological phenomena that occur when a person is on the verge of death or recovering from a critical situation. For decades these facts were kept hidden by the patients themselves, for fear of being labeled mentally ill. For its part, officially, the medicine of the time looked for organic causes that could be consequences of the original trauma itself.

However, little by little NDE have aroused the interest of many researchers and scientific disseminators, who have tried to explain their causes, consequences and meaning. Some of the main scientific works and videos on NDE are:

- **Life after life, by Raymond Moody**. It is the pioneering book that coined the term NDE and collected the testimonies of hundreds of people who had experienced them.
- **The Proof of Heaven**, by Eben Alexander. It is the personal story of a neurosurgeon who suffered an NDE after meningitis and who changed his vision of consciousness and spirituality.
- **What Happens When We Die?**, by Sam Parnia. It is a scientific study that analyzes the medical and neurological evidence of NDEs and their implications for the understanding of the mind and brain.
- **The tunnel of death, from Documentos TV**. It is a documentary that explores NDE from different perspectives, including testimonies, experiments and theories.
- **The science of near-death experiences**, by Mario Alonso Puig. It is a conference that addresses NDE from an integrative approach, combining neuroscience, psychology and philosophy.

These are just some of the best-known references and surely not updated, since in this field of knowledge there are numerous works that are published every day..

2.1.1 Some of the most significant characteristics of NDE

In any case, it is worth highlighting some of the most significant characteristics of NDE, which are reported in the literature, especially the following::
- Feeling of peace and tranquility.
- Separation from the body and perception of floating or flying within the room; passing from one space to another without difficulty, until emerging into space, as a bird flies.

- Vision of a bright light or a dark tunnel, which each patient characterizes with their personal vision
- Meeting with deceased loved ones or spiritual entities.
- Life review and moral evaluation, which the patient views as if it were a screen, and everything happens in a few seconds, although to the subject it usually seems like an indeterminate amount of time.
- Change in human perspective and own values after recovery.

The list is expanded depending on the author, but there is a notable correspondence with the situations listed. One of the most solid and disseminated opinions, especially through scientific and public conferences, interviews for television programs, etc., are those of **Dr. Manuel Sans Segarra**, professor of *General and Digestive Surgery*, at the *Bellvitge University Hospital*, in Barcelona, one of the most recognized people in the field today. Along with him, stands out **Dra. Luján Comas**, Anesthesiologist and Researcher, president of the *ICLOBY Foundation*, an institution that was born as a result of its founder **Xavier Melo Bulbena**, who suffered an NDE.

The fundamental purposes of this foundation are the dissemination of knowledge and research based on empirical sources related to the State of Consciousness at the time of cardiac arrest. It is considered one of the most advanced institutions in these studies, which also teaches different types of Master's and postgraduate courses for specialists related to Medical Sciences.

For those culturally interested in the topic, we especially recommend the Scientific Documentary "*Near Death Experiences. Information for Health Professionals*", produced by the *ICLOBY Foundation*, for the LUZ Project, and can be located at the address

https://www.youtube.com/watch?v=jwWcamj4WK8

As its name indicates, it is an audiovisual designed for Health personnel, in general, not familiar with NDE and their derivatives, and in fact for the general public, on the basis of erasing certain unfounded beliefs. , according to which NDEs can be understood by objective explanations such as:

- Neurological alterations caused by lack of oxygen, stress or medications, causing hallucinations in the sick or injured person.

- Projection of consciousness outside the body as a form of psychological defense.
- Manifestation of the spiritual or transcendent dimension of reality, associated with the subjective Illusion generated by cultural or personal expectations.

It has been precisely the public interventions of Dr. Manuel Sans and Dra. Luján, which have contributed, with arguments that make one think, that NDE cannot be explained as a reason for hallucinations and psychological factors, considering, among other factors, that The reasons that usually motivate hallucinations are well studied, they are not repetitive, but rather specific to specific individuals, and they are quickly forgotten in the course of days, and even hours.

According to Sans and Luján, NDE are unrelated to causes related to hallucinogenic diseases, stress or other factors of possible psychiatric origin.

In our opinion, and there are not many that I assume as my own in this work, having dismantled such arguments has been the first of the most notable advances, within the works investigated in relation to NDE. Because once this has been achieved, the path is clear to necessarily look in other directions, and in all cases the objects of study must consider the Neurosciences and the most recent and notable results obtained by Quantum Mechanics.

Recent news

However, a recent press report on developments in NDEs states that researchers at Stanford University have resolved the mystery, and disclose that A group of neurologists led by **Dr. Josef Parvizi** have discovered that an area of the brain called Medial Parietal Cortex (PMC) is responsible for the sensation of "escape from the body" that people who have had an NDE experience. According to Parvizi, the PMC helps create what is known as our "narrative self," a A kind of internal autobiography that helps us define who we are, but we have not been able to locate a single link to direct sources.

In the aforementioned article he also comments that this phenomenon is also related to the effects that ketamine produces in the brain, and acts in a similar way to electrical brain stimulation, but at the moment we cannot expand on the details of the news.

2.1.2 Other important considerations in relation to NDE.

NDEs can have a profound impact on the person experiencing them, as well as their family and friends. Some positive consequences of NDEs are:

- Greater appreciation for life and the present.
- Less fear of death and greater acceptance of it.
- Greater compassion, altruism and empathy towards others.
- Greater interest in personal and spiritual development.

However, NDEs can also cause difficulties in adapting to everyday life, such as:

- - Feelings of isolation, misunderstanding or guilt.
- - Conflicts with religious beliefs or social values.
- - Problems relating to others or to one's own body.
- - Depression, anxiety or post-traumatic stress.

Therefore, it is important that people who have had an NDE receive adequate psychological and emotional support, as well as truthful and respectful information about this phenomenon.

2.1.3 Other disciplines with direct links to NDE

There are several areas that study and research near-death experiences (NDEs):

- Medicine: Doctors and scientists study the physiological processes that occur during an NDE, such as brain activity, hormonal changes, among others. They seek to understand what happens in the body during these events.

- Psychology: Psychologists analyze the psychological effects of NDEs, such as changes in personality, attitudes towards life and death, possible traumas, etc. They also study the experiences perceived during the NDE.

- o **Psychiatry**: Psychiatrists explore possible neurochemical or brain explanations for NDEs. They analyze whether they may be due to hallucinations, dreams or drug effects.
- o **Parapsychology**: Parapsychologists investigate whether NDEs can evidence paranormal phenomena or the existence of a soul/consciousness separate from the body.
- o **Religion**: Various religious traditions analyze NDEs according to their beliefs about life after death and the soul. Some see them as evidence of a spiritual existence.
- o **Philosophy**: Philosophers contemplate questions about the relationship between mind and body, mortality, the meaning of life, raised by NDE testimonies.

In summary, NDEs are studied from multiple academic and spiritual perspectives, given the depth of the questions they raise about life and death.

2.2 Reincarnation

If we go specifically, regardless of the variety of opinions on the matter, it can be summarized that Reincarnation is the belief that the soul or consciousness of a person can survive physical death and be reborn in another body, whether human (or animal), to continue their spiritual evolution, and many etcetera.

However, as (Kloppenburg, B, 1993) clarifies, there is no unanimity of criteria regarding Reincarnation, nor among its own followers. There are great differences between reincarnationists from the East (India, China, etc.) and those from Western Europe.

According to the same author, in Europe, reincarnationist ideas are initiated by in France, during the years from 1830 to 1848, especially in certain socialist environments closely linked to the principles of evolutionism, then in fashion. The following quote abounds in details in this regard.

"The "codifier of Spiritism", known by the pseudonym "Allan Kardec", was called Denizard Hippolyte León Rivail, born in Lyon in 1804 and died in Paris in 1869. As all his books were published under the pseudonym Allan

Kardec, will be cited with this name. His type of Spiritism is, therefore, also known as "Kardecism" or "Kardecist" Spiritism, to distinguish it from others such as the Anglo-Saxon that do not admit reincarnationist philosophy.. (Kloppenburg, B, 1993:11).

The list of all his works is as follows:

I. The Book of Spirits (1857), 22a. Brazilian edition.

II. What Spiritism is (1859), 10a. Brazilian edition.

III. The Book of the Mediums (1861), 20a. Brazilian edition.

IV. The Gospel according to Spiritism (1864), 39a. Brazilian edition.

V. Heaven and Hell (1865), 16a. Brazilian edition.

VI The. Genesis (1868), Brazilian edition of 1949.

VII. Posthumous Works, 10a. brazilian edition

Another key personality in the spiritualist context, with a solid history related to reincarnation, is **Edgar Cayce**. Throughout his life, this psychic performed more than 14,000 readings, or so-called psychic discourses, on a wide variety of topics. Of these, approximately 2,500 are what have been called life readings, that is, readings that refer to the previous incarnations of the person being consulted (Amith, R, s/f)

This idea is part of many Eastern religions such as Hinduism and Buddhism, but has also been defended by some Western philosophers such as Plato and Pythagoras. Additionally, there are documented cases of children remembering past lives with verifiable details that cannot be explained by chance or suggestion.

Returning to the concept, in a very summary way, so as not to commit ourselves to a matter that has conflicting criteria, we can say that, according to Wikipedia, "Reincarnation is the belief that the soul or consciousness of a person can be reborn in another body after of death".

Following a chronological logic, it would be natural to have begun this work precisely with Reincarnation, since the origins of such a belief are ancestral, and are part of the culture rooted in the origins of many human groups.

But it happens that this work does not go in that direction, nor are we giving a logical historical treatment to its contents. The belief in reincarnation has been present throughout humanity since ancient times, in most eastern religions, such as Hinduism, Buddhism and Taoism. and not so in those of Judeo-Christian origin, where its practice exists but is manifested through means considered heretical.

In fact, we start from the base and previous knowledge of some notable works in the treatment of this topic, focusing on basic aspects that could serve generic knowledge for the reader we are writing about, who is above all Western and probably with religious beliefs in the that reincarnation is not accepted as part of beliefs, and there are also different denominations to identify conceptions that allude to the existence of a soul or spirit that appears in different bodies, as part of a personal evolution towards a perfection of the being; and a learning that provides earthly existence, until reaching a higher state of consciousness.

In reality, the bibliography on the subject is very extensive, but for the objectives mentioned for this work, an extension can be widely found by the reader in the work "All about reincarnation" which is a kind of manual, without references to the compiler, but carried out by New Acropolis Spain, which brings together in more than 300 pages a collection of articles that deal with various aspects linked to the knowledge of Reincarnation.

We are interested in focusing on the results of relatively recent research, developed by psychiatrist **Ian Stevenson**, working for more than 40 years on numerous reports of children who claimed to remember a past life. These works were developed at the University of Virginia, with a tradition in paranormal studies. He had a long life, and that allowed him to publish various works.

Stevenson received private donations that allowed him to make multiple trips to carry out his research on reincarnation, studying cases in Africa, Alaska, Europe, India, and North and South America, etc. He reported that the children he studied normally began to talk about their supposed past lives between the ages of two and four, but stopped doing so around the age of seven or eight, in many cases mentioning having died a violent death, with clear memories of how in which they died.

But these efforts by Stevenson did not correspond with the acceptance of his work at the academic level, such as the philosopher Paul Edwards, who included an extensive criticism of Stevenson's works in his book Reincarnation: A Critical Examination, in a context where it already prevailed. scientism, although Stevenson's research is associated with a "minimalist" model of reincarnation, which makes no religious claims.

Another widely known author is Brian Weiss, American psychiatrist, famous for his controversial beliefs in reincarnation, past life regression, future life progression, and the survival of the human soul after death, authoring several books on these topics. , among them one of the best known is "Many lives, many teachers", his first work, published in 1988, which had a notable impact on the public.

2.2.1 Is there a relationship between NDE and Reincarnation?

•   The possible relationship between NDEs and recorded cases of reincarnation have been the subject of study and research by various authors and disciplines, both from the scientific and spiritual fields.

•   Without giving absolute credit, and even out of curiosity, we have consulted the ChatBot Claude, asking the question posed by this section, and in the answer the following hypotheses are given:

•   NDEs would be a form of contact with the spiritual plane that is accessed after physical death and from which one can be reincarnated into a new existence.

> NDEs would be a manifestation of the soul's memory or consciousness that transcends the body and can retain memories of past or future lives.

•   NDEs would be a projection of the beliefs, expectations and desires of the person experiencing them, which may be influenced by their culture, religion or education and which may reflect concepts about reincarnation.

- The NDEs and the recorded cases of reincarnation would not have any causal relationship between each other, but rather would be independent phenomena that respond to different psychological, biological or paranormal factors and mechanisms.

Currently, in a context where research is disseminated at an unusual speed, and the public often finds out about a result before the specialists themselves, there is information available to fill, on Reincarnation, the pages that the whole of this work does not have...

We can, however, add some comments that allow the reader to know aspects of the matter, which are less discussed at the level of popular scientific text. For example:

• Science has not been able to prove or disprove the existence of reincarnation, but there are some researchers who have explored this phenomenon from different perspectives. Every day there is more evidence that confirms the relevance of NDE studies, and correspondingly, the certainty of a post-life incarnation, with many questions to be answered between life and life.

• Statistical analysis of birthmarks and congenital deformities related to supposed past lives, carried out by doctor Ian Stevenson, found a significant correlation between both factors in some cases.

• Past life regressive hypnosis, practiced by psychologist Brian Weiss and other therapists that we will discuss in the next point, consists of inducing the patient to remember experiences from their supposed previous existences for therapeutic purposes.

  • The theory of biocentry, proposed by the physicist Robert Lanza, which states that consciousness is the foundation of reality and that it is not extinguished with the death of the body, but is transferred to another level of existence (Lanza, R , 2023).

In the work Biocentrism: How Life and Consciousness are the Keys (BenBella Books), the American physicist starts from the premise that life creates the universe, and not the other way around, the very basis of biocentrism. *"Death, as we conceive it, does not exist, it is only an illusion."* This is the conclusion reached by Robert Lanza, director of Advanced Cell Technology

From here Lanza deduces step by step that mortality is a false idea, created by our conscience. Published by Iván Gil. There is life after death, but "our *mind does not see* it."

https://www.elconfidencial.com/alma-corazon-vida/2014-01-13/la-fisica-demuestra-que-hay-vida-despues-de-la-muerte-pero_74673/

It is clear that the topic continues to be a point of attention for authors and researchers. Furthermore, many minds are focusing attention on the results that the nascent Neurosciences will provide in the coming years.

2.2.2   The "Reincarnation" of Bridey Murphy

To partially close this topic, because it will inevitably be present in other content of this work, we are going to dedicate a few paragraphs to commenting on "The Story of Bridey Murphy" popularized by the book "The Search for Bridey Murphy" by Morey Bernstein. To some extent it remains an interesting case in the study of reincarnation.

As narrated in (Kloppenburg, B, 1993). Its author was an honest businessman from a town in Colorado (U.S.A.), 35 years old, who dedicated himself to hypnotism as a hobby, despite not being a specialist.

In the work, Berstein recounts a regression session held with Virginia Tighel, achieving the revelation of detailed data about her alleged previous life, lived in the last century in Ireland under the name Bridey Murphy.

We are not going to tell the story, which was told in various media of the time, causing an extraordinary communication impact, to the point that a young man committed suicide, with the intended purpose of verifying the experience personally.

We intend to take a look back in time, when more than 60 years have passed since the publication of the work. Some researchers suggest that Bridey Murphy's case could be an example of cryptomnesia, where forgotten memories resurface without the person being aware of their origin. This implies that the details of Bridey Murphy's life could have been subconsciously remembered by Virginia Tighe (the hypnotized woman) from past experiences and not necessarily from a previous life (Swanc, B. 2020).

The story became a public investigation, because when comparing regression data with reality facts, inconsistencies were found that could only be justified if the situation was analyzed as a case of cryptomnesia, which occurs in the subconscious of the hypnotized person. .

The psychologist **Martin Gardner** has said of all this:

> *"Almost any hypnotic subject capable of entering a deep trance will babble about a previous incarnation if the hypnotist asks him to do so. He will babble just as freely about his future incarnations. In every such case in which a proper verification of the subject's past has been made, it has been discovered that the subject was weaving together fragments of long-forgotten information acquired during his early years."* (Swanc, B. 2020).

The complete history of what was discussed can be consulted at the address;

"The Mysterious Reincarnation of Bridey Murphy", by Brent Swancer, March 26/2020. https://mysteriousuniverse.org/2020/03/the-mysterious-reincarnation-of-bridey-murphy/

Even today, no conclusions have been reached about the veracity or deception regarding this story, which is due to gossip and nonsense that always surrounds the mysteries, and not infrequently promoted by ill-intentioned people who make the context their own to sow poison and extract their own benefit while distorting stories, making the work of science difficult.

In order not to leave the reader who does not know the final details on tenterhooks, we transcribe below the last part of the article by (Swanc, B. 2020), which we have taken as a source. According to Swanc:

> *"Less kind skeptics have accused the case of being pure fabrication and deception orchestrated by Virginia and Bernstein for fame and money. For his part, Bernstein staunchly defended himself against his critics, and was quick to point out that simply having an Irish aunt and a causal relationship with a neighbor when he was very young and whom he didn't even remember, did not translate into the incredibly profound Virginia's knowledge of 19th century Ireland. (…)*

> *For her part, Virginia Tighe would deny having had any interest in Ireland, much less 19th century Ireland, and claimed to have had no exposure to it in any way, certainly not enough to provide all the obscure details she had*

provided. . He also did not pursue any fame or money from his situation, and aside from a few interviews, he lived largely under the radar and out of the spotlight until his death in 1999. (…)

There are many things that she undoubtedly took to the grave with her. Was she really the reincarnated form of a 19th century Irish woman? How could he know all the things he knew? Was it just a clever ruse, and if so, did she set up Bernstein or was he involved too? Even decades later, the case of Virginia Tighe and her alter ego, Bridey Murphy, remains unexplained, and is one of the great reincarnation cases, still disputed to this day."

If we are allowed to take sides in this debate, since we have brought it to these pages, we consider that time will surely have answers, when science has the latest technologies for this. Maybe **J.J. Benítez**, or his follower, give us a story, on a trip to the past, in the style of Trojan Horse, with new lights and above all, the verification of truths; but we take it for granted that the truth will not be the confirmation of a fraud constructed by the protagonists.

2.2.3 Most important experiences recognized by Science.

Currently, as we have already commented, the sources with validable information in relation to the phenomenon of reincarnation are growing, but every day it is more difficult to validate the facts, because in all directions the danger of fraud of all kinds also increases. . In this scenario, and without the commitment of having to provide new data, we limit ourselves to summarizing the most significant ones in the known bibliography. Let us then mention the following cases:

- The case of Shanti Devi, an Indian girl who remembered her past life as Lugdi Devi, a woman who died in childbirth. Her memories were verified by Lugdi's husband and son, as well as several researchers, including Mahatma Gandhi.
- The case of James Leininger, an American boy who remembered his past life as James Huston Jr., a World War II pilot who died in combat. His memories coincided with historical data and with the testimonies of Huston's relatives and companions.

- The case of Cameron Macaulay, a Scottish boy who remembered his past life on the island of Barra, where he had a family and a white house near the sea. His memories were confirmed by his biological mother and by the inhabitants of the island, whom he visited with a television crew.
- The case of Jenny Cockell, an English woman who remembered her past life as Mary Sutton, an Irish woman who died leaving eight children. His memories allowed him to locate his reincarnated children and establish contact with them, which was documented in several books and television shows.
- The case of Swarnlata Mishra, an Indian girl who remembered her past life as Biya Pathak, a woman who died of kidney disease. Her memories were corroborated by Biya's husband and friends, as well as the doctor who treated her. Furthermore, he showed signs of xenoglossia, that is, the ability to speak a language unknown in his current life.

2.3 Regressions through hypnosis

The previous story serves as an introduction to formally dedicate an epigraph to specifically comment on regressions to the past, even to previous lives, through hypnosis.

One of the applications of hypnosis is regression, which consists of taking the person back to previous stages of their life, and even to past lives, to resolve traumas or unresolved conflicts. Therefore, it starts from accepting that reincarnation exists. Hypnosis allows you to access a person's subconscious and modify their memories, beliefs or emotions.

Regressions are a technique that consists of inducing the patient into a state of deep relaxation, similar to sleep, in which they can access past memories that are normally hidden or repressed in their conscious mind. Hypnosis is the most used method to facilitate Regressions, as it allows the hypnotist to guide the patient through their memories and help them explore them safely and without external interference (Weiss, 1988).

In theory, if it is accepted as a theory, hypnosis essentially occurs by working on the levels of consciousness (**conscious, subconscious** and **supraconscious**), usually in the intermediate plane, the subconscious plane of the person. To speak of the supra conscious is to cross the epistemological barrier, which is illustrated in figure 1, in the initial pages of this work. That is, to deal directly with concepts that move within the current limits of science, a barrier that every day is more threatened by the discoveries of Quantum Mechanics, at least.

Regressions can have several objectives, such as resolving traumas, phobias or emotional conflicts, recovering forgotten skills or talents, learning about past or future lives, or simply satisfying personal curiosity (Newton, 1994, 2000).

Regressions are not dangerous or harmful, as long as they are performed with a qualified and ethical professional, who respects the patient's limits and pace, and offers adequate support before, during and after the session.

According to several authors, regressions can be a very valuable tool for self-knowledge, personal growth and healing, as long as they are done with an open, honest and responsible attitude. But it is clear that in our case, as authors, we cannot make judgments, much less deny the information. We are not judges, in any case chroniclers.

Some well-known examples of regressions through hypnosis are:

- As we already know, one of the applications of hypnosis is regression, which consists of making the person go back to previous stages of their life, and even to past lives, to resolve traumas or unresolved conflicts (Moody, 1975).
- The case of Virginia Tighe, another American woman who under hypnosis remembered having been an Egyptian princess named Ra-ab. His story was also published in a book and generated controversy due to the supposed historical evidence it provided (Tighe & Bernstein, 1956).
- The case of Dolores Cannon, a hypnotherapist who developed a technique called QHHT (Quantum Healing Hypnosis Technique) that allowed her to access the past lives of her clients and obtain information about the origin of the soul, the purpose of life and the future of humanity (Cannon, 2010).

2.3.1 How is a hypnotic regression performed?

The process varies depending on the method and the professional who applies it, but in general a similar scheme is followed:

A hypnotic regression is a therapeutic method that uses hypnosis to access memories from the past that may be causing problems in the present (Wright, 2022). The process typically involves the following steps (Cunningham, 2009):

Preparation

The therapist explains the hypnotic regression process and establishes a relationship of trust with the client. Expectations are discussed and informed consent is obtained.

Hypnotic induction

The client is guided into a hypnotic trance state using techniques such as progressive relaxation and focus on breathing. This allows you to increase suggestibility and access the subconscious.

Regression

Once in trance, the therapist guides the client to relive and re-experience a specific past event, often from childhood. The client may be encouraged to observe the event as an external spectator.

Prosecution

During and after the regression, the therapist helps the client process emotions and perspectives related to the event. This can lead to new understanding and integration.

Reorientation

Before ending the session, the client is gently guided back to the present. This completes the regression process.

Follow-up

In subsequent sessions, the therapist and client discuss the meaning of what was remembered and how to apply its essence to current problems.

2.3.2 Some authors who have published on regressions

Obviously the list could be innumerable in these pages, nor is it covered by our knowledge, in terms of having criteria for each person's works. But it is enough to comment on the best known, and I wish we could summarize the works of all of them. Let's get started:

- **Brian L. Weiss**, author of "*Through Time,*" a book that explains hypnosis as a technique for accessing past life memories.
- **Horacio Ruiz Iglesias**, author of "*Practical Guide to Hypnosis: From Basic Techniques to Regression*", a book that teaches the scientific and theoretical foundations of hypnosis, as well as practical exercises to practice it.
- **Sigmund Freud**, who was the first to propose that hypnosis enables access to the unconscious, although he later replaced hypnotic regression with evocation in a waking state.
- **Michael Balint**, **John Bowlby**, **Bruno Bettelheim**, **Donald Winnicott** and **Ronald Laing**, among others, who proposed the use of regression as an instrument that allowed a new "*paternal reeducation*" more satisfactory than the original.

Some of the works that Michael Balint published on regressions are:

- **The basic lack**: Therapeutic aspects of regression. In this book, Balint develops the concept of basic lack, which originates in the initial period of life due to the discrepancy between the needs and care of the child. This lack affects the dyadic realm of the mind, formed by the individual and its primary object, and can lead to a regression in the analytical situation. Balint proposes a therapeutic technique based on acceptance and primary love to treat these cases..
- **Regression:** what it is according to psychoanalysis (and criticism). In this article, Balint distinguishes between two types of regression: a benign one, which occurs in childhood or in artistic creation, and a malignant or pathological one, which is related to neurosis and schizophrenia. Balint considers benign regression to be a way of expressing primary narcissism and the desire for harmony with the

environment, while malignant regression is a defense against Oedipal conflict and external reality.

In a parallel line, Robert Schwartz and his memorable work *"The Plan of Your Soul"* cannot fail to be mentioned. The work is about the planning that each soul does before incarnating on Earth. Some of the central topics it addresses are: El proceso de planificación pre-nacimiento: Schwartz explica, a través de casos de sus clientes, cómo el alma elige a sus padres, el lugar y el momento de nacer, los retos y obstáculos a superar, con el fin de aprender lecciones y cumplir misiones de vida.

o Soul Contracts: details how we make agreements with other souls, before we are born, to find and support each other, or to play out specific roles of antagonists or growth catalysts.
o Choice of gender, sexual orientation, disabilities: the soul decides these aspects before incarnating for the lessons and experiences they will bring.
o Karmic influences: past lives and the need to repair errors or continue processes started previously shape the pre-birth plan.
o Spiritual guides: angelic beings who advise the soul in the planning phase and care for it during its physical incarnation.
o The purpose of life: know and fulfill the mission or tasks that we have come to carry out in this life.

In conclusion, the work provides a deep vision about the meaning of our existence based on the pre-birth planning of the soul. Offers answers to existential questions about suffering and challenges experienced.

2.4 The Medium unit

Giving a definition of this term is quite complex. To give a definition of terms that could be questionable in the academic context, it is necessary to make a commitment of conditional acceptance without demonstration. In this case, we can say that it is accepted that a Medium or clairvoyant (which is a quality and not a characteristic) is a person who seems to have the ability to communicate with the spirit of a deceased person or with other entities on the astral plane.

The medium acts as an intermediary between the physical and spiritual worlds, transmitting messages, information or energy. The medium can enter a trance state, in which his consciousness moves away to make way for that of the spirit that communicates through him, or he can remain conscious and perceive the psychic impressions he receives. Mediumship (or messianism) is a spiritual practice that is based on the belief that there is a continuity of life after death and that it is possible to establish contact with departed loved ones.

According to the book codified by Kardec, A. (2019) **"The Book of Mediums"**, it is proposed that from the moment the existence of the soul and its individuality after death is admitted, it is also necessary to admit that it is of a different from the body, since once separated from it it no longer has its properties; It enjoys being conscious of itself, otherwise it would be an inert being. Admitted this, the soul goes somewhere; What does it become and where does it go? According to common belief, he goes to heaven or hell, but where are heaven and hell? (Kardec, A., 1996)

According to this work, spirits communicate through mediums, who serve as instruments and interpreters; and it is also stated that mediumunity is an inherent faculty of the human being, but not everyone develops it or uses it correctly.

There are different types of mediums, depending on the mode of manifestation of the spirits, such as mediums of physical effects, auditory mediums, psychic mediums, psychographic mediums, among others..

Mediumship is a gift that must be used responsibly and charitably, following the principles of the Gospel. In an article titled "Spiritism x Spirituality: Main differences in Kardec's vision on the Spiritist Content website, the difference between spiritualism and spirituality is explained and presents the basic principles of Spiritism according to the vision of Allan Kardec..

2.4.1 Actions that a medium can perform.

Following Kardec's ideas, in Kardec, A. (2019), it is possible to group the actions that a medium can generally perform, into the following:

- Rituals, prayers, invocations or cleansing to protect oneself, harmonize the environment or help souls in their transition.

- Offer advice, guidance, healing or comfort to people seeking to contact deceased loved ones or resolve pending issues.

- **Channeling**: It consists of transmitting the messages or energy of a spirit through the voice, writing or gestures of the medium. The medium can enter a trance state or maintain consciousness during the process.

- **Clairvoyance:** It is the ability to perceive visual information about the past, present or future that is not available to the normal senses. The medium can see scenes, symbols, colors or figures related to the spirit or the situation consulted.

- **Clairaudience**: It is the ability to hear sounds, voices or music that come from the spiritual plane. The medium can receive direct auditory messages from the spirit or pick up environmental sounds that give clues to its presence or intention.

- **Clairsensitivity:** It is the ability to physically or emotionally feel the vibrations, emotions or sensations of the spirits or of the people involved in the consultation. The medium may experience cold, heat, pain, joy, sadness or any other feeling associated with the spirit or the consultant.

- **Psychometry**: It is the gift of obtaining information about a person, a place or an object by coming into contact with it or with something that belongs to it. The medium can access memories, impressions, emotions or relevant data about the origin, history or destiny of what he examines.

These are some of the most common actions that a medium can perform, although there are others that are more specific or less frequent. Each medium has its own skills and ways of working, so no two are the same. The practice of mediumship requires adequate preparation, ethics and responsibility to avoid fraud, deception or harm to the spirits or the consultants.

2.4.2 Differences between spiritualism and mediumistic unity.

These are some of the most common actions that a medium can perform, although there are others that are more specific or less frequent. Each medium has its own skills and ways of working, so no two are the same. The practice of mediumship requires adequate preparation, ethics and responsibility to avoid fraud, deception or harm to the spirits or the consultants.

https://conteudoespirita.com/es/espiritismo-x-espiritualidad/
https://www.larazon.es/viajes/20200410/wckjpe2eubgvvmbydjrdoilpzm.html.

- Spiritualism is based on the principles and teachings of Allan Kardec, who compiled and systematized the revelations of higher spirits in several books, such as The Book of Spirits, The Book of Mediums, The Gospel According to Spiritism, etc. Spiritualism is considered a science, a philosophy and a religion, since it studies the nature, origin and destiny of spirits, the moral laws that govern life and human progress, and the existence of God as the first cause of all. things. consulted in;
https://es.wikipedia.org/wiki/Espiritismo, https://concepto.de/espiritismo/ y
https://conteudoespirita.com/es/espiritismo-x-espiritualidad/

- The manifestation of life after death can have different origins, sources, methods and purposes, depending on the culture, religion, tradition or current to which they belong. Some may be based on sacred texts, others on personal experiences, others on ancestral rites, etc. Some may aim to know the future, others to heal illnesses, others to honor the deceased, etc.

2.4.3 The perspective of death according to different cultures

It is a very interesting and diverse topic. Each culture and religion interprets the meaning of death and what will happen after life in its own way. Some examples of how death is lived and celebrated in different parts of the world are:

- In Mexico, the Day of the Dead is a popular festival that combines pre-Hispanic and Catholic elements, and consists of honoring the deceased with offerings, altars, flowers, sugar skulls, music and food. González, A. (2019) See:
https://www.larazon.es/viajes/20200410/wckjpe2eubgvvmbydjrdoilpzm.html

- In Africa, Lumbalú is a funeral ritual practiced by the Afro-Colombian community of Palenque, which has its roots in African traditions.

- In Buddhism, death is considered a transition to a new rebirth, which depends on the karma accumulated by the individual in their previous lives. Pérez, M. (2015)

These are just some examples of how death is conceived and expressed in different cultures and religions.

2.4.4 Who have been the most famous mediums in history

Out of simple curiosity, we have consulted the Copilot Artificial Intelligence module (we also plan to do it with others, but not for this book) about the 20 most famous mediums that existed, and the list presented is the following.

RELACIÓN DE MEDIUMS MÁS FAMOSOS DEL MUNDO – Según Copilot				
Nombre	País	Fecha de Nac.	Fecha de Fall.	Características de su método
John Edward	EE.UU.	19/10/1969	19/10/1969	Psychic readings, communication with spirits
James Van Praagh	EE.UU.	23/08/1958	23/08/1958	Psychic readings, communication with spirits
Theresa Caputo	EE.UU.	10/06/1966	10/06/1966	Psychic readings, communication with spirits
Allison DuBois	EE.UU.	24/01/1972	24/01/1972	Lect. psíquicas, colaboración con fuerzas de la ley
Lisa Williams	Reino Unido	19/06/1973	19/06/1973	Psychic readings, communication with spirits
Gordon Smith	Reino Unido	06/07/1962	06/07/1962	Psychic readings, communication with spirits

Tyler Henry	EE.UU.	13/01/1996	13/01/1996	Psychic readings, communication with spirits
Matt Fraser	EE.UU.	08/07/1991	08/07/1991	Psychic readings, communication with spirits
Kim Russo	EE.UU.	12/06/1964	12/06/1964	Psychic readings, communication with spirits
Thomas John	EE.UU.	08/05/1984	08/05/1984	Psychic readings, communication with spirits
Char Margolis	EE.UU.	21/08/1951	21/08/1951	Psychic readings, communication with spirits
Rebecca Rosen	EE.UU.	07/11/1975	07/11/1975	Psychic readings, communication with spirits
Maureen Hancock	EE.UU.	05/12/1968	05/12/1968	Psychic readings, communication with spirits
Laura Lynne Jackson	EE.UU.	27/07/1973	27/07/1973	Psychic readings, communication with spirits
Sally Morgan	Reino Unido	20/09/1951	20/09/1951	Psychic readings, communication with spirits
Derek Ogilvie	Países Bajos	24/02/1965	24/02/1965	Psychic readings, communication with spirits

Mavis Pittilla	Reino Unido	15/03/1947	15/03/1947	Psychic readings, communication with spirits

2.4.5 Brief biographies of some of the currently active mediums

Below is the list of the best-known mediums, who remain active to date.

John Edward

John Edward is an American psychic medium born October 19, 1969. He is known for his television show "*Crossing Over with John Edward*," where he performs live psychic readings and connects people with their deceased loved ones. Edward has written several books about his experiences and methods, and is renowned for his ability to provide specific details during his readings. Her approach focuses on direct communication with spirits and delivering messages of comfort and closure to her clients..

James Van Praagh

James Van Praagh, born August 23, 1958, is an American medium and author. He is known for his television show "*The Ghost Whisperer*" and for his numerous books about life after death and communicating with spirits. Van Praagh uses his ability to see and hear spirits to provide detailed and accurate readings. He has worked in television and radio, and is a frequent speaker at spiritual and self-help events.

Theresa Caputo

Theresa Caputo, born June 10, 1966, is an American psychic medium famous for her television show "*Long Island Medium*." Caputo claims to have the ability to communicate with spirits from a young age and has used this ability to help people connect with their deceased loved ones. His readings are known to be emotional and detailed, and he has written several books about his experiences and methods.

Allison DuBois

Allison DuBois, born January 24, 1972, is an American medium and author. She is known for being the inspiration behind the television series "*Medium*," which is based on her experiences working with the police to solve cases. DuBois claims to have the ability to communicate with the dead and to foresee future events. He has written several books about his skills and experiences, and continues to offer readings and lectures.

Lisa Williams

Lisa Williams, born June 19, 1973 in the United Kingdom, is a psychic medium known for her television shows "*Lisa Williams: Life Among the Dead*" and "*Lisa Williams: Voices from the Other Side*." Williams claims to have the ability to communicate with spirits and has used this ability to help people find comfort and closure. He has written several books and offers workshops and live readings around the world.

Gordon Smith

Gordon Smith, born July 6, 1962 in the United Kingdom, is a psychic medium known for his accuracy in readings and his ability to provide specific details. Smith has appeared on numerous television and radio programs, and has written several books about his experiences and methods. Her approach focuses on direct communication with spirits and delivering messages of comfort and guidance to her clients.

Tyler Henry

Tyler Henry, nacido el 13 de enero de 1996 en Hanford, California, es un médium psíquico conocido por su programa de televisión "*Hollywood Medium with Tyler Henry*". Henry afirma haber descubierto sus habilidades clarividentes a una edad temprana y ha utilizado estas habilidades para proporcionar lecturas a celebridades y personas comunes. Ha escrito un libro titulado "*Between Two Worlds: Lessons from the Other Side*" y continúa ofreciendo lecturas y apariciones en televisión.

Matt Fraser

Matt Fraser, born July 8, 1991, is an American psychic medium known for his television show "*Meet the Frasers*." Fraser claims to have the ability to communicate with spirits from a young age and has used this ability to help people connect with their deceased loved ones. She has written a book titled "*When Heaven Calls*" and offers live readings and workshops around the world.

Kim Russo

Kim Russo, known as "*The Happy Medium*," is an American psychic medium famous for her television show "*The Haunting Of...*". Russo claims to have the ability to see and communicate with spirits from a young age. He has written several books, including "*The Happy Medium*" and "*Your Soul Purpose*," and offers live readings, workshops, and lectures..

Thomas John

Thomas John, born May 8, 1984, is an American psychic medium known for his television show "*Seatbelt Psychic*." John claims to have the ability to communicate with spirits and has used this ability to provide detailed and accurate readings. He has written a book titled "*Never Argue with a Dead Person*" and offers live readings and workshops around the world.

2.5   Spiritual Channeling

Spiritual channeling is understood as the act of connecting with a high-vibration being of light to receive their guidance and messages. We call spiritual guides high vibrational light beings, who can be angels, archangels, ascended masters or people who have passed away and gone to the light, among others.

Of course, to accept this definition, one must first renounce any personal conception that denies spiritual realities; But those researchers who seek to seek any philosophical truth must also renounce their faith.

When we talk about high vibration, we are referring to the energy that the being or person in question has and transmits. Those who transmit love, joy, peace and plenitude vibrate high. The connection with them helps to balance and feel those emotions (Sánchez Montalbán, A. (s/f)

Therefore, they are not the author's words, but we give credibility to what was said, and with this we also give space for any response that opens a debate from critical positions.

Let us then accept what has been said: spiritual channeling occurs when a person connects with a spiritual guide and listens to his message, to capture it in written form, orally or through music, painting or any other artistic manifestation. Projects, advice, instructions, recipes, techniques for performing various functions, books, paintings, songs and, in short, everything that is necessary and appropriate for the person receiving the message can be channeled. Therefore:

- Spiritual channeling is the process of contacting universal energy, teachers, angels and guides, beings of very high vibration, who can offer information of a spiritual, emotional, creative nature, etc. See: https://spiralaurea.com/blog-evolutivo-espiritual/que-significa-canalizar-mediumnidad-e-intuicion
- Mediumship is a form of spiritual channeling that consists of communicating with beings who have died, who can help find answers, comfort and guidance. See: Spiritual Channeling and Mediumship Course - The World of Minerva.

  https://elmundodeminerva.com/curso-canalizacion-espiritual-y-mediumnidad.

- Intuition is another form of spiritual channeling that involves listening to the inner voice, the heart or the soul, which can give certainties, hunches or ideas that cannot be explained with reason. See:

  https://spiralaurea.com/blog-evolutivo-espiritual/que-significa-canalizar-mediumnidad-e-intuicion

- All human beings have the ability to channel, but some have it more developed than others. You can work on channeling through different techniques and tools, such as meditation, tarot, pendulum, etc.
- Spiritual channeling can have benefits such as deepening intuition, being a light guide for other people, changing lives forever, and regaining soul

vision. See: https://spiralaurea.com/blog-evolutivo-espiritual/que-significa-canalizar-mediumnidad-e-intuicion

- Spiritual channeling can also have risks if it is not done with respect, ethics and discernment. One can fall into deception, manipulation or dependence on the entities or channeled messages.

2.5.1 Are we all capable of doing spiritual channeling?

En un artículo firmado por Valeria Joaniquet, diplomada en aroma terapia emocional. (Joaniquet, V., s/f) se resumen los siguientes aspectos de interés

Todos los seres humanos somos receptores potenciales, o sea canales, como si tuviéramos una antena en nuestro interior, que nos permite absorber esa clase de información que no pasa a través de los sentidos físicos.

Algunas personas tienen como preferente el canal receptor visual (imágenes), otras puede que «escuchen» frases o palabras en su mente, y hay quienes la sienten como emociones o síntomas en el cuerpo. En definitiva todos somos capaces de recibir canalizaciones espirituales.

- **Difference between Channeling and Medium**

  The topic of spiritual channeling can be confused with the work of mediums or psychics, although only in some cases, clairvoyance and channeling occur at the same time. What differentiates one medium from another is that in spiritual channeling, information is always received from beings that are not in a physical body.

  The entities that contact us to assist us from unconditional love (that is, without asking for anything in return, or demanding something from those who consult) are Guides or Teachers who have reached a level of wisdom greater than ours, and are in another dimension, from which they can have access to another level of information.

- **Conscious spiritual channeling**

  Not all channelers (or people who claim to be channelers) have the same intention when offering themselves as such. For a pipeline to be reliable, some points should be taken into account:

- The information provided will never violate the privacy of those who are present or that of third parties, that is, answers should not be given that could interfere with the lives of others whether they are present at that moment or not, and never without your consent.

- The information should never condition the person who requests it, telling them what they have to do and what they should not do. Nor is resentment, anger or rage encouraged by agreeing with a conflict, since that does not fall under "unconditional love" and is very different from giving support or support to someone who suffers for some reason.

- The energy that is perceived goes beyond the words that the channeler can say, and love, dedication and an enveloping and comforting presence can be felt.

  - Words know where they have to touch: directly to the heart. The person who receives them may feel indifferent because they are closed or defensive, because the logical thing is that they move us, since they go to the depths of our being, and always with compassion and love.

En un punto están de acuerdo diferentes autores, y es que solo se necesita el deseo de escuchar al propio guía espiritual, al que muchos llaman **ángel guardián o ángel de la guarda**, y la voluntad de confiar en los mensajes que se van a recibir. La ayuda de un guía espiritual es fundamental para encontrar el sentido de la propia vida y desarrollar le propósito que nos trajo aquí.

2.6 Instrumental Transcommunication

Ernest Senkowski, born in Hamburg in 1922, was a pioneer in the concept of "Instrumental TransCommunication" (T.C.I) and worked since 1976 in this field. as an experimental physicist. He died in 2015.

There are two types of communication, mediumistic communication, decoded by Alan Kardec in 1857, which is the ability of people to feel, listen, see and write the spiritual world), and instrumental communication, which arises over the years. '20 with the creation of electronic devices.

This topic could seem like "*a point outside the curve*," as mathematicians point out when they want to highlight that an aspect is outside of what is being discussed, even though it is part of it, being a sign that "*something*" is being discussed. escaping the occurrence of a detail, or an incomplete measurement, etc.

But it is not an irregular theme at all, quite the opposite. It could become the direct communication route between "**the here**" and "**the beyond**" that a group of specialists are looking for. Because precisely what we want is to fine-tune the dial of communication, only it is said that among the specialists "**from beyond**" who are working to achieve this, there is none other than Tesla himself!.

It is, therefore, a component of the problem, which even the most convinced believers and the most serious impartial researchers, seen from faith, do not see clearly, because we are talking about the fact that there are means of telecommunication between the living and the dead. . And if that were not enough, it is not ruled out that this route or possibility of communication, in certain frequency bands (or better, high frequency) is shared with extraterrestrial beings: a true **MIXED EVERYTHING** that we already announced as a hypothesis in the opening chapter of this work.

It is difficult to follow a beaten path when trying to write general ideas, because it is a field where several interrelated definitions are integrated, such as **psychophonies, paraphonies, electronic voice phenomena**, which are sounds of electronic origin recorded in audio recorders and received. very diverse interpretations.

In general terms, it is proposed that communication is the exchange of information between two interlocutors who influence each other. Ordinary communication occurs through the sensory organs in an immediate environment, modernly expanded thanks to the technique and various devices invented for this purpose. Extraordinary communication occurs outside the organic sense organs and is called telepathic or paranormal. In the scientific field, this type of communication has not been accepted because it lacks theory, a measurable carrier, and it lacks the ability to transform the concept of space-time. However, in recent decades, the number of scientists involved in researching these phenomena has multiplied, and some reputable universities have departments dedicated to these phenomena..

2.6.1 The origins

That is why it is convenient to start by doing a little history. The most accepted is that the promoter or casual discoverer was an artist, documentary producer and opera singer, named Friedrich Jürgenson, born in Estonia on February 8, 1903.

Everything happened in the following way. During the summer holidays of 1959, while he was with Monica, his wife, in the countryside, he tried to record the song of the finch bird to make a documentary. For this purpose, he set up a small tape recorder near a forest outside his house and remained silent while the sound of the birds was recorded on the device, taking several shots. He later listened to the tape inside the house, and began to listen to what was recorded. The audio was clear and the chirping of the birds could be heard perfectly, but he found that in the recording someone apparently imitated the chirping of the birds, spoiling the shot, and then heard the voice of someone speaking in Norwegian, making comments about the chirp of the finch. He discarded the recording, thinking that someone had entered the area where he was, without Jürgenson realizing it. The next day he repeated the recording operation, in the same area, taking care that no one walked within several tens of meters of the device, and again, when playing the recording, along with the song of the finch, a new voice could be heard perfectly, but on this occasion he thought he recognized the voice of his deceased mother, telling him something that only they knew: the affectionate and familiar name his mother called him: Friedel... my little Friedel... Can you hear me? Taken from: Wikipedia 2017.

From then to the present, investigations have been numerous and with diverse objectives, because only with verifiable information is it possible to obtain the agreement of the academic media.

According to Chivo Xavier, the famous Brazilian medium:

Mediumship is demonstrated by experimentation, in different ways. Credulity in the phenomenon is not enough; Therefore, all methods were used to confirm the veracity of the messages received. Aside from cases of fraud, confusion or ignorance, it was possible to verify that the spiritual entities that claimed to be present established without a doubt their identification, and their messages were consistent with their personality known in incarnated life.

Generally, those who deny this experience do so a priori, based on their previous beliefs that would be distorted if spiritual communication were proven.

Michael E. de Bakey stated:

"The natural history of science is the study of the unknown. If you fear the unknown, then you will not study it and you will not make any progress." Many deny it without knowing the experiments carried out by multiple scientists in different areas of knowledge, which confirm it."

The set of hypotheses included in Wikipedia (2017) is interesting, in relation to the different explanations that the literature includes about this phenomenon..

2.6.2 Hypotheses that attempt to explain the supposed phenomenon

There are almost as many as there are researchers, although there are some more accepted than others.

- **Subliminal / unconscious ventriloquism** - This is one of the first explanatory theories of the supposed phenomenon. The theory in question assures that psychophonies are voices of the researchers themselves that involuntarily move the vocal cords and larynx, producing sounds that are imperceptible among those present but that are recorded in the recording device. It's a theory that has become less popular over the years.

- **Radioelectric interference - Psychophonies**, or at least some of them, are explained as a result of radioelectric interference with the recording device. Psychophonies have been obtained using recording devices installed inside Faraday cages, which largely cancel out radioelectric interference, but not completely. Traditionally, this argument has been used to rule out the possibility that radio interference is the origin of some psychophonies, although in practice Faraday cages are not a perfect shield against interference and the argument is weakened.

- **Sounds from beyond / voices of the dead** - This is the most widespread theory, especially among the general public. Its weak point is that it is pseudoscientific, since it is based entirely on religious beliefs and hypotheses that are unproven or unprovable by their very nature.[

- **Parallel dimensions** - they could not only be sounds produced by deceased entities, but also thought forms, which would act as entities with a certain intelligence without ever having consciousness.

- **Inhabitants of other planets** (aliens) - It is one of the least considered theories, but it has a certain number of researchers who firmly believe in this explanation. It is comparable to the previous one.

- **Performance of the investigator's mind or psychokinesis**.. It is another of the most widespread theories. It would be a mental emanation at a conscious or unconscious level on the part of the researchers and that would act on the matter (recorder, microphone...). It is not specified what kind of emanation it is, nor is the specific mechanism by which the sounds would be recorded described. In this sense, the term psychophony, composed of the words "psycho" (mind) and "fonia" (sound), alludes etymologically.

- **Pareidolia** - Pareidolia is a phenomenon that consists of the interpretation of a vague and random stimulus as something recognizable and ordered. It is the phenomenon that makes us perceive recognizable shapes in the clouds and intelligible words in our language in songs sung in a different language, for example. The noise in a recording can be interpreted as voices, screams and other sounds associated with human activity without necessarily being real.

- **Fraud** - In a topic given to pseudoscientific speculation, with the consequent lack of control implied by the non-application of the scientific method, the possibility of fraud cannot be ruled out in some cases and for various reasons. Psychophonies taken for granted seem to be nothing more than a mere fraud reproduced by crude means, such as that of the famous "Ghost of the Granada Provincial Council", as can be seen in a video on the Internet.

- **Voices in the air and echoes of the past** - Other theories given to this phenomenon is the possibility that all the waves we emit are stored in the air, are trapped or bounce in space, and thus, when a researcher starts recording, captures those waves that are recorded on the tape or recording device.

- **Standing waves** - That which states that sound waves can be trapped in time and recorded after the event occurred; It is similar to the previous one.
- **Environmental or energetic impregnation** - it is proposed that living beings or certain situations leave a trace or energetic imprint, being recorded in space-time, in another plane of reality (interphase).

It is curious that so much technology is at the service of research that is technically carried out as if everything were being studied in a normal laboratory context, but it turns out that the researchers are working with colleagues, who are in the afterlife!

In recent years the most interesting results that have been disclosed by various sources are:

- Starting in 2015, independent work begins, such as in Seattle, where Simone Santos creates applications that reproduce the voices of spirits on electronic devices.
- On the other hand, in Milan, Italy, a special sensitive camera is developed that captures the ectoplasm of the medium in trance and the spiritual world, now beginning to capture images, shadows, faces that are more defined and possible to identify.
- In Sao Paulo, Sonia Rinaldi, with 30 years of study and research, dedicated herself to studying spiritual communication and discovered that there are three spiritual stations through which spirits communicate today.
- The technology of invisible beings surpasses us in quality and time, they are engineers from the spiritual world who develop advanced technology to be able to communicate with us, proving in a real way that the death of the physical body does not end life.

2.7   The Akashic Records

According to Hindu tradition, the Akashic records are the archives of the soul's memories. It is not a physical space of this dimension, but an energetic one, without measurements of time (there is no yesterday or today), where the archives that contain the history of all existence are kept.

For believers in this tradition, opening the records is entering the soul to understand the reason for the things that happen to us and growing based on that.

But in the next pages we will see a different and novel version, which makes the Akashic records a source of information that goes beyond what was assumed until recently, thanks to the theoretical conclusions of Dr. Bruce Lipton (Lipton, B ., s/f).

However, we will accept that the Akashic records are an esoteric concept, which refers to a spiritual repository of all knowledge and history, both personal and universal, which can be accessed by applying certain techniques.

We can summarize that some key ideas about the Akashic records are:

- They are believed to contain all the information about the past, present and future of an individual and the universe.

- They are described as a "*library*" on the spiritual or dimensional plane that records all experience.

- They are supposedly accessible through meditation, intuition or working with psychic mediums.

- Its existence has not been scientifically proven. It belongs more to esoteric and spiritual traditions.

- In practical terms, accessing these records is generally done as part of a healing process that the person undergoes, whether for therapeutic or spiritual reasons.

Some notable authors who have written on these subjects are:

- **Edgar Cayce** – Medium and "father of the new age," promoted the Akashic records in his psychic readings.

Cayce, E. (1968). The outer limits of Edgar Cayce's power. doubleday

- **Rudolf Steiner** – Founder of anthroposophy, described them as a "cosmic ether" that records everything.

  Steiner, R. (1971). An outline of esoteric science. Anthroposophical Press.

- **Helena Blavatsky** – Theosophical leader who claimed the soul can read records in higher states of consciousness.

  Blavatsky, H. P. (1888). The secret doctrine: The synthesis of science, religion, and philosophy (Vol. 1). Theosophical Publishing Company.

- **James Van Praagh** – Contemporary medium who claims to channel the Akashic records. Van Praagh, J. (2002). Talking to heaven: A medium's message of life after death. NALTrade.

- **Lisa Williams** - Medium who wrote the book "The Akashic Records: Access to Ancestral Knowledge and Wisdom."

  Williams, L. (2019). Accessing the akashic records: Exploring the archive of the soul and its journey. Hay House, Inc

Although there is no scientific consensus, these authors have popularized and spread the concept in esoteric and spiritual currents..

2.7.0 The research of Scientist Jacobo Grinberg

Jacobo Grinberg was a prominent Mexican neurophysiologist and psychologist who dedicated himself to studying the phenomenon of consciousness from an interdisciplinary perspective that integrated science and shamanism. Among its most relevant contributions is the **Syntergic Theory**, which proposes that reality is a matrix of information that can be modified by the human mind through processes such as telepathy, meditation and healing.

According to Martínez González, "*Jacobo Grinberg's syntergic theory proposes that there is a continuous space of energy and that the common human can only perceive a part of it. The result of this process is what everyone understands as "reality.*" (Martínez González, R. (2007). "*What shamanism left*

50

us: one hundred years of shamanic studies in Mexico and Mesoamerica."
Anales de Antropología.)

As far as is known, The Syntergic Theory was born from his work with Bárbara Guerrero, considered a Mexican psychic and healer known as **Pachita**. Grinberg was intrigued by Pachita's reputation as a psychic healer, so he followed her procedures for about a year. He came to the conclusion that Pachita's ability to heal was the result of two different realities: on the one hand, the presence of a neural field that surrounds our brains and, thus, the presence of a spatio-temporal network, which is combined with Einstein's conception of spacetime. (Jorge Caballero, J.]] (2023). Sintergia, "*homage to my father, who left a scientific legacy*": Estusha Grinberg. La Jornada, March 15, La Jornada de Enmedio, p. 12a, Entertainment section.

https://www.jornada.com.mx/notas/2023/03/15/cultura/sintergia-homenaje-a-mi-padre-que-dejo-un-legado-cientifico-estusha-grinberg/__Consulted Saturday, March 18, 2023).

However, the majority of scientists who have been interested in verifying the facts narrated by Grinberg about Panchita consider that her ability to heal is a fraud, even though Grinberg's research on the transfer of potential in the brain was published in Physics Essays magazine,

Grinberg carried out numerous experiments to test his theory, based on the scientific method and contact with Mexican shamans such as Pachita, who is said to have performed paranormal surgeries with a kitchen knife. Grinberg wrote more than 50 books about his research, but mysteriously disappeared in 1994, leaving a legacy of knowledge and mystery about the nature of human consciousness.

But behind all this it seems that there is something more than mystery, as we will see in the paragraphs that follow.

In short, we venture to comment that Grinberg carried out numerous experiments to verify his theory, in his studies on the brain, making it at the same time more complex, in an interrelation between science and paranormal phenomena, as if it were not already complex enough with the presence of Quantum Mechanics.

That is, we are talking about the extreme disclosure of Grinberg's relationship with the paranormal phenomena associated with Mexican Shamanism, in the person of Pachita, (Bárbara Guerrero) the "blind" old woman who, practically doing "black magic", performed operations even with an open heart, Grinberg being the one who brings out of anonymity, the "miracles" of the Mexican healer, by narrating these events in his work.

But the matter is not at all clear. Recently, Pachita's granddaughter, **Liliana Ugalde**, spiritual follower of Cachita, has declared that most of the miracles attributed to her grandmother, through the work of Grinberg, are false. They are strong, solid, credible statements that cast destroying the credibility of the scientist's work. ("Debunking Books and Myths of Jacobo Grinberg" at https://www.youtube.com/watch?v=1a1laEn7U1A)

In that interview Liliana ratifies her grandmother's Curandera condition, which included what she calls "spiritual surgery," but she flatly denies that the procedure included surgery with knives, and replacement of organs with others that appeared in her hands in a inexplicable, as Grinberg relates in the works he dedicates to narrating the grandmother's methods. He also complains about the number of videos with false information that have proliferated on the Internet in recent years, with falsehoods of all kinds, such as revealing that Pachita was blind, and absurd stories narrating false cures that never occurred.

It is true that, since she was a child, she had powers for spiritual healing. There is a whole known story about it, but this is not the place to comment on it. If we can say that, according to various references that Liliana confirms, the one who really performs the healings, acting as Pachita or her granddaughter as a medium, is the spirit of Cuauhtémoc, 'the Little Brother', who was the last Mexica tlatoani of Tenochtitlan. Equivalent to Emperor of the Aztec Empire. He assumed power in 1520, a year before the taking of Tenochtitlan by Hernán Cortés and his troops.

You can now understand how much cultural wealth exists behind each of these sources, waiting for poetry to discover them...

The truth is that, taking these facts as a reference, miraculous or not, Grinberg develops his Syntergic Theory, which, working at the level of consciousness, is combined with aspects of Quantum Mechanics. There are experiences narrated by direct participants of such *"miracles", who remember* "at higher levels of consciousness it is possible to materialize and dematerialize objects. Pachita did it when she performed transplants at will, healing and remote diagnosis with incredible power and accuracy. *"He was capable of knowing the thoughts, intentions and intimate experiences of his collaborators and patients."* Cited in The Power of Pachita and the Syntergic Theory, by Jorge Salazar García, in

https://www.google.com/url?sa=t

We will return to some of these aspects in the next chapter of this work.

2.7.1 Grinberg and the Fifth Dimension.

First of all, it is necessary to clarify certain points that may be incomprehensible to many readers.

According to Wikipedia, in physics, a sequence of N numbers can be understood to represent a place in an N-dimensional space. When N = 5, it can be called **the fifth dimension**. Five-dimensional abstract space occurs frequently in mathematics, and is perfectly constructible. If the real universe is 5-dimensional, this can be explored in many branches of physics such as astrophysics and particle physics.

Quantum Mechanics is the branch of Physics that studies the behavior of subatomic particles and the laws that govern the universe on a microscopic scale. This theory has revolutionized our understanding of reality and has raised numerous enigmas and paradoxes that defy common sense and classical logic. Some of these phenomena are the uncertainty principle, quantum entanglement, the observer effect, superposition of states, and parallel universes.

We know that Jacobo Grinberg is a Mexican scientist and researcher, transformed into a journalist as a popular disseminator of his own work, who has dedicated himself to studying and disseminating topics related to paranormal phenomena, quantum physics, extraterrestrials and topics highly questioned by science. His work is based on extensive bibliographic and testimonial documentation, as well as on his own personal experience as a witness and protagonist of some of these phenomena. Grinberg, in addition to his many books and articles, has participated in radio and television programs both in Mexico and in other countries. But... we already know that there have been hidden letters of her disappearance, which Pachita's granddaughter casts doubts on.

Paranormal phenomena are those events or manifestations that cannot be explained by known natural laws or by conventional science. Some examples are telepathy, clairvoyance, precognition, psychokinesis, levitation, bilocation, mediumship, poltergeist, instrumental transcommunication, cryptozoology and parapsychology. These phenomena suggest the existence of hidden capacities and dimensions in human beings and in the universe.

What relationship could exist between all these topics? A possible answer is that they all point to the same underlying reality that transcends space and time, and that implies a deep connection between consciousness and matter, between the visible and the invisible, between the individual and the collective, between the human and the divine. A reality that invites us to expand our vision of the world and ourselves, and to explore the infinite possibilities that the cosmos offers us..

But according to Grinberg, "*If the fourth dimension is the eternal present, the fifth is human relationships.*" This quote appears in different works without giving the exact reference, but there is no doubt that bigger things are being talked about here. Because behind this expression his ideas related to his work on Transferred Potential already emerge, directly linked to his studies in Telepathy.

In the introduction to the work "*The Transferred Potential*", a degree thesis supervised by Grimberg, the author states that "*Transferred Potential (TP) has been called a brain potential recorded in a non-stimulated subject, similar and synchronous to a provoked induced in his partner with whom he has previously interacted.*"

Reference is being made here to one of the experimental works developed by Grinbert and his team, in the laboratories of the UNAM, Mexico, most likely the last of his works, before his mysterious disappearance.

It is not tacitly said, but it is clear that the unstated foundation can be found in Quantum Mechanics.

The quote continues with: The transferred potential has the characteristic of presenting itself only when a "*direct communication*" was established between the subjects, non-verbal empathic communication, meditation. (Grinberg-Zylberbaum, De la flor, Sánchez, Guevara, & Pérez, 1992).

It is not necessary to go deeper. We are only interested in presenting our readers with evidence that in 1992 concrete steps were already taken with a view to scientifically substantiating that Telepathy is a communication process between two brains, which in our days agrees with the quantum processes associated with the concatenation between two entities, whose demonstration earned the Nobel Prize in Physics in 2022.

It can be said that PT is a potential caused by the activation of a distant brain. The transferred potential has the characteristic of presenting itself only when a "*direct communication*" was established between the subjects, non-verbal empathic communication, meditation. (Grinberg-Zylberbaum, Delaflor, Sánchez, Guevara, & Pérez, 1992).

In an unreferenced press article, published at https://invdes.com.mx/ on July 30, 2022, the main idea is summarized and the aforementioned experiment is described, which we reproduce literally, because being a journalistic text, it hits good for readers interested in knowing, at least in their basic elements, the results achieved by Grinberg.

Grinberg is perhaps the first scientist who unified science with spirituality, claiming that there is a hypercomplex structure of energy to which we are connected and which he called 'lattice'.

By the time of his disappearance, in 1994, it was unthinkable for a renowned scientist like Jacobo Grinberg to address these issues, even though other disciplines had already reached similar conclusions.

But in a world governed by the physical laws of beginning and end, his research seemed dangerous and some of his texts were discredited. Almost 30 years later, an openness to consciousness has allowed him to resume his work.

2.8.0 Jacobo Grinberg's last experiment

Jacobo Grinberg worked rigorously, had the support of Conacyt and had a laboratory at UNAM where, before mysteriously disappearing, he developed what was his last experiment: transferred potential.

This was what the Mexican scientist called communication between brains. His goal was to demonstrate that our perception is what creates the reality we experience.

And, along the way, the main thing for Jacobo Grinberg was to verify that there is potential transferred between brains. To do this, I chose couples with an emotional connection, whether love or friendship.

He put each of them in a room isolated from electromagnetic frequencies (so that nothing interfered with the result), blindfolded them, sat them facing each other and asked them not to talk.

What they could do was think about each other, until they felt a connection. Immediately afterwards, Jacobo Grinberg took one of them out and took him to another isolated room quite a considerable distance from the previous one.

The idea was that people would be further away from each other and without communication.

Gentlemen, if this is not quantum concatenation, what else can it be...?

As Grinberg explained, this connection is amplified when there is an emotional relationship between individuals, and the information shared between brains is called transferred potential.

One of the most enthusiastic experts with the work of Jacobo Grinberg was the Indian-North American scientist Amit Goswami, a quantum physicist – of whom we have already commented since the Introduction – with whom, through a satellite and thousands of permits, the Mexican would carry out its Mexico-India experiment.

Other important scientists of the time said that the reality is that everything is connected, and this is one of the laws of quantum physics.

That is, reality is not separated from the observer. And if this is so, then each of us affects and creates our reality.

2.8.1 Lattice. Poetry in mental waves …

A theory that Grinberg proposed to explain the interaction between mind and matter is Lattice, which is based on the idea that the universe is composed of a network of information that connects all beings and phenomena. According to Grinberg, this network is the substrate of reality and can be modified by the conscious intention of individuals. Thus, the Lattice would be the means by which paranormal phenomena can be produced, such as telepathy, clairvoyance or psychokinesis.

We can add that Psychokinesis is the supposed ability to move or influence physical objects with the power of the mind, without the intervention of any physical agent. It is a paranormal phenomenon that has been the subject of study by parapsychology, but no scientific evidence has been found to support it. Some examples of psychokinesis are telekinesis, pyrokinesis, cryokinesis, and electrokinesis.

Grinberg conducted several experiments to demonstrate telekinesis, that is, the ability to move objects with the mind. One of them was the one he did with the healer Pachita, whom he observed operating with her bare hands supposedly with the help of the spirit of Cuauhtémoc. All of this is well documented, and also falsified, depending on the sources. Even Grinberg himself has been questioned by Pachita's granddaughter, as we have already mentioned in these pages.

Grinberg recorded the brain waves of Pachita and his patients during the operations and found a synchronization between the two. According to Grinberg, this indicated that Pachita could manipulate matter with her mind and transfer information to her patients. It turns out that this agrees with the studies of **Bruce Lipton**, which we will expand on in the final section of this chapter, which, as we will see, have also received as many or more unfavorable criticisms than Grinberg,

But we also know that it is very difficult to separate, like oil and water, where scientific truth prevails, and where personal or even institutional interests prevail. Only serious research and with the indispensable infrastructure resources will be able to open the way to new paradigms, in the style of Thomas Kunt (Kuhn, T. (1971), a product of the ever-present epistemological problems of demarcation. (Kuhn, T. (1971); Páez, Andrés (2008); Open the door to the reader who wants to delve deeper into the background of what he or she is reading.

In fact, Grinberg did not limit himself to the topic of the questioned "*surgical interventions of Cachita*" – which, by the way, in the times of Cortés' Mexico were understood by the Spanish of the conquest as "*human sacrifices*", and today, from another perspective, are being studied to determine if they were really misinterpreted Aztec healings – but he also worked on an experiment he planned to do, with the aim of establishing telepathic communication between a person in Mexico and another in India, challenging Einstein's theory of relativity. . However, this experiment was never carried out, as Grinberg mysteriously disappeared in December 1994, leaving no trace or explanation, but one unknown: Was he alive, working in an unknown dimension?

2.9.0 Do donors "speak" through recipients?

When the work was practically completed, my dear friend and collaborator, **Lic. Orlando Rubén Licea Díaz**, was working on closing the editorial review and realized that a topic as controversial as the possible exchange of cellular information between a donor and a recipient patient, in organ transplants, was being forgotten.

It is good to comment now that having the collaboration of Professor Licéa has not only been important, but has been an honor, for several reasons. After many years of work as a clinical psychologist, specialized in the therapy of Asthma (without the use of medications), he received the National Research Award, also supported by the publication of several books and personal care for thousands of patients, through the Asthmatics without Asthma page, located on the Facebook platform. But also, it will not be a merit, but it is worth noting that he is the only person I know who is a survivor of a fairly complex NDE.

Looking for a name that would typify this epigraph, it is strange that its content does not appear more frequently related to the phenomena that we have presented in the work. That is why we have highlighted the Donor-Patient relationship as essential, which really is "*suigeneris*", because everything indicates that it is for life.

Summarizing as much as possible the information that we have managed to specify, to at least not fail to approach the main part of the problem, we can relate the following.

One of the most referenced authors is **Dr.Paul Pearsall**, from USA, PhD at Harvard and the Albert School of Medicine Einstein. Dr. Pearsall, who also received a transplant, is a psychoneuro immunologist, that is, a psychologist who studies the relationship between the brain, the immune system and our experiences of the outside world. He has experience of more than thirty years of scientific practice in the interpretation of how external events influence our health. But he is especially known for being the author of the book "The Heart's Code: Tapping the wisdom and power of our heart energy. Broadway Books", published in 1999, translated into Spanish as The Code of the Heart.

Considering the authors mentioned, some of the most significant facts reported are the following:

- There are some documented cases of transplant recipients who appear to acquire memories, preferences, or personality traits from their deceased donors. However, the scientific evidence in this regard is limited and controversial.

- One study found that 47% of heart recipients reported personality changes that they attributed to their donors' cellular memory (Pearsall, 1999). But the study has methodological limitations.

- A widely cited case is that of a young woman who, after a heart transplant, had dreams that allowed her donor's murderer to be identified. But critics point out inconsistencies in the case (Pearsall, 1999).

- Researchers suggest that these effects may be due to psychological factors such as recipients' propensity to feel a connection to their deceased donors (Burton, 2012).

- From a scientific perspective, there is no evidence that memory can be stored in organ cells and transmitted in transplants (Sharp, 2021).
- More controlled research is needed to determine the validity of these reports of cellular memory transfer (Carter, 2021).

One of the most cited cases about the possible transfer of cellular memory in transplants is that of Claire Sylvia, reported in the aforementioned book "The Heart Code" by Paul Pearsall.

- Some details about this case that could be relevant for a scientific article:
- Claire Sylvia received a heart and lung transplant in 1988, at age 47.
- According to reports, after the transplant she had cravings and impulses that were very out of the ordinary for her, such as a taste for beer, spicy chicken and motorcycles.
- Later she met her donor's family and learned that he liked those same things.
- He also claims to have had information about the donor that only his family knew, such as his death by suicide with a firearm.
- The case has been presented as evidence of cellular memory transferred in the transplant.
- But critics point out inconsistencies in dates and details between Claire's version and the donor's factual information.
- From a scientific point of view there is no reliable verification of the supposed memory transfer.
- This case, although controversial, can be useful in a scientific article as an emblematic example of the claims about cellular memory in transplants and the scrutiny they deserve from a skeptical point of view. Provides illustrative details for analysis.

There is a significant aspect that is not reflected in what was seen above, and it has to do specifically with the heart, as a vital organ. in a web article published by Emma Anselmi, June 25, 2010, on the page https://misteriosdenuestromundo.blogspot.com/2010/06/el-cerebro-del-corazon-parte-ii.html. in which the author begins by characterizing the importance that the great cultures of humanity gave to the heart, as the center of the soul.

He thus points out that "The Greeks were aware that the heart was the source of life, and that the various aspects of life - the centers of consciousness called the "*gods*" - dwelt in the heart."

The author recounts the vision that various cultures have of the heart, but what is interesting to highlight is that this relates it to the inexplicable events that have been reported in heart transplants. He especially mentions the author of one of the few books that today collects these experiences. He refers to Claire Sylvia, author of the work "*A Change of Heart*", where the changes experienced by the author as a result of a transplant operation are narrated. .

And here we have saved a surprise to conclude this brief comment on the possible exchange relationships at the cellular level between a donor and the recipient: It turns out that Paul Pearsall, author of the other work mentioned, was also the subject of a heart transplant...

2.10.0   The discoveries of Bruce LIpton

For the author, encountering the work of **Dr. Bruce Lipton** was a true discovery, which led directly to a no less important discovery, and that is knowing the work of the quantum physicist Heinz R. Pagels, author of the book "*The Code of the Universe.*" : a language of nature."

Lipton is an American cellular biologist, born in 1944, known for being a proponent that genes and DNA can be modified by a person's beliefs (Lipton, B., 2007).

This idea in itself is revolutionary and oppositional, since it polemicizes diagonally with the concepts established in genetics: it is not genetics that absolutely determines the genesis of the being, but even beliefs can determine genetics and its descendants. Hence, the reading of the Akashic records can assume an origin that is not necessarily spiritual, and that is why those who work in that field are looking with more interest today at the results of science, when theories such as Bruce's allow us to consider that history The totality of an individual is recorded in their own genes, and therefore, having access to that information can be of extraordinary importance in a healing process.

According to Dr. Lipton's own website, in 1982, he began examining the principles of Quantum Physics, and how they applied to his understanding of the information processing systems of the cell. He conducted groundbreaking studies on the cell membrane, which revealed that this outer layer of the cell was an organic counterpart to a computer chip, the cellular equivalent of a brain.

His research at Stanford University School of Medicine, between 1987 and 1992, revealed that the environment, operating through the cell membrane, controlled the behavior and physiology of the cell, turning genes on and off.

Dr. Lipton's discoveries, which contradict the established scientific view that life is controlled by genes, gave rise to one of the most important fields of study today: the science of Epigenetics, which refers to the study of all non-genetic factors that intervene in determining the development of an organism.

As the specialist himself explains, the novel scientific approach also transformed his personal life. His deeper understanding of cellular biology highlighted the mechanisms by which the mind controls bodily functions, and he applied this science to his personal biology and improved not only his physical well-being, but also the quality of his daily life (Lipton, B. , 2007).

As explained in García-Giménez, J.L. (2012), following the completion of the Human Genome Project in 2001, scientists have realized that there is much more to the molecular basis of cellular function, development, aging, and many diseases. The idea that was had a few years ago that human beings and other organisms are only what is written in our genes from their conception, is changing, and science is advancing to decipher the language that encodes small chemical modifications, capable of regulate gene expression.

The theme is like a Pandora's box in the 21st century, but we already know that the objective of this small work is not to go further along almost unknown paths of science, but to show that in that world of questions, there is virgin space for creation in arts and literature.

But we are going to leave some interesting ideas, captured in Lipton's work, that do go in the direction we are exploring.

Let's start with his own website, where as an introduction Bruce tells us point blank:

What would your life be like if you knew you were more powerful than you have been taught? (Bruce, L). https://www.brucelipton.com/es/

Having disdained Quantum Mechanics in his days as a Biology student had a lot to do with his own life, but such opinions were clearly overcome when he clarified in his original work that:

"For those of linear thinking, I will clarify that we have officially returned to quantum physics, through which I learned that scientists will never understand the mysteries of the universe using linear thinking alone. (Bruce, L., (2007: 74)

And to be more definitive he then states that:

"Physics, after all, is the basis of all sciences, although we biologists rely on the outdated but more orderly Newtonian version of how the world works. We stick to Newton's physical world and ignore Einstein's invisible quantum world, in which matter is actually composed of energy and in which absolute terms do not exist. From the atomic point of view, matter does not even exist exactly; it just has a tendency to exist. All my certainties regarding biology and physics had been shattered!" *(Bruce, L., (2007).*

Today, many years later, scholars of the Akashic records have seen in the work of Bruce Lipton a path through which to explore the mysteries of the human mind, but with our feet placed in nature itself, which perhaps we are just beginning to understand. discover.

With such perspectives, it is worth completing this incomplete overview of Bruce Lipton's research – because we have only mentioned one of his important works – including the following quotes:

- "By changing our way of living and perceiving the world, we can change our biology." Cited in:

  https://www.espaciocodigodeluz.es/somos-lo-pensamos-vivimos/

- "The mind is energy. When you think, you transmit energy, and thoughts are more powerful than chemistry. *"Beliefs themselves become an energy field, a transmission, and this is transformed into a signal that is capable of changing the organism.*
  "https://diariolaopinion.com.ar/contenido/73239/perotti-y-karina-rabolini-en-santa-fe

2.10.1   Critical opinions on the works of Bruce Lipton

Being a theory with so many edges, it is logical to assume that on all fronts it must have received the most conflicting opinions.

According to the information available, the theory of the Biology of Beliefs is considered revolutionary in the field of modern Biology. This theory proposes a change in the understanding of the influence of DNA on people's destiny. Some key points about the Biology of Beliefs are:

- The Biology of Beliefs was developed by cell biologist [Bruce Lipton] (https://www.google.com/search?q=Bruce%20Lipton). His book "*The Biology of Belief: Liberating the Power of Consciousness, Matter, and Miracles*" is an important work in this field. From there we extract some considerations.

According to this theory, our beliefs and thoughts can influence the expression of our genes and our overall health. It is argued that the environment and the signals we receive can activate or deactivate certain genes.

The Biology of Belief proposes that our beliefs and perceptions can have an impact on our biology at the cellular level. It is argued that our emotions, thoughts and attitudes can affect the way our cells function and communicate with each other.

This theory suggests that our beliefs can influence our health, well-being, and success in life. It focuses on the importance of mind and consciousness in human biology.

However, it is important to keep in mind that the Biology of Beliefs has been the subject of debate and criticism in the scientific community. Some scientists believe that more research and evidence is needed to fully support this theory.

Let's look at some arguments that should not be ignored..

a) **Scientific debate:** The Biology of Beliefs has been the subject of a continuous scientific debate. Some scientists argue that the claims made by the theory are not supported by sufficient empirical evidence and that more rigorous research is needed to validate its claims (Novella, S, 2007).

b) **Complexity of genetics:** Critics point out that the relationship between beliefs and genetic expression is much more complex than theory suggests. The influence of multiple factors, such as genetic inheritance, environment, epigenetics, and other mechanisms, makes the relationship between beliefs and biology difficult to determine precisely (Massey, D. S., 2016).

c) **Simplistic interpretation:** Some argue that Belief Biology may oversimplify the complexity of biology and genetics. They point out that the theory does not take into account all the variables and biological processes involved in genetic expression and regulation (Flamm, B., 2007).

d) **Lack of solid empirical evidence:** Although there is some scientific support for certain aspects of the theory, such as the impact of stress on health, some critics argue that there is a lack of solid empirical evidence and rigorous studies supporting the broader claims of the Biology of Stress. Beliefs (Dresser, N, 2007).

e) **Possible bias and pseudoscience:** Some detractors consider that the theory of the Biology of Beliefs may have elements of pseudoscience and that the statements made by its defenders may be based on biases or erroneous interpretations of scientific evidence (Offit, P, 2008) .

It is important to note that these critical views do not completely invalidate the Biology of Belief theory, but highlight the need for rigorous scientific evaluation and greater empirical evidence to support its claims.

In summary, the Biology of Beliefs is a theory that proposes a change in the understanding of the influence of DNA on people's destiny. Although it is considered revolutionary by some, it has also generated debate and criticism in the scientific community..

Chapter III

Death in poetry seen from a perspective of hope

3.1.0 Death does not know how to kill[1]

Certainly the title of the chapter seems a contradiction, because in all the variants in which it usually appears, death does not agree in any way with hope, but quite the opposite: as a rule it is associated with the absolute loss of the last breath of hope.

And for similar reasons, this first epigraph, for the first time in history, declares de facto that death is innocent. It happens that we have entered the contact zone, between life and death, where poetry reigns.

But the author has not written this work for pleasure, linked to death from beginning to end. And here we are not talking about death, but about life after death. We are not saying goodbye to a duel, but we are creating a context where poetry and literature in general have arguments to continue loving beyond death, to continue living, beyond the ephemeral life, without it being technically impossible, and at best a poetic license.

Said and done, if the new discoveries of Science serve at least to sow doubt about death, technically they open the doors to a more credible literature, without changing a letter between before and after, but allowing a total opening to creativity, sustainable in accepted truths.

And to these truths is added a qualitative hypothesis: if we are energy that oscillates depending on our creative, discursive or negative activity, the pleasure that our activity produces increases its frequency, while routine minimizes it. Therefore, on an energetic level, a simple poem that sensitizes our mind, as a certain melody can also do, produces in the interrelation between the human psyche and the work, a pampsychist effect with positive influence.

We can include a simple example here, inspired by the text we are writing. If we accept to put the existence of reincarnation in the judgment of doubt, with 70%

---

[1] Titulo de un poema del autor, que al mismo tiempo es el título del poemario de igual nombre.

certainty for any statement we make, I - in first person - could tell the reader, that I have well-founded suspicions, that my spirit - is say my eternal Soul - comes with a Karma of ancestral incarnations as a writer, and that is why I feel so much strength when and it is even easy for me to construct the arguments that support it.

By the way, I can add – still in the first person – that in my poetic or narrative work, death is usually just another character, who always has a mission to fulfill, but nothing to do with that terrifying death, which everyone fears.

And "*my Self*" or whoever it is, sees things differently.

In my poetic work, which is otherwise quite unknown, it usually happens that death (as a fictional character) arrives at the moment of death – logically, it could not be otherwise – but with the function of certifying the death (delivering the deceased the authorization to move on to the next life) although for relatives, etc., etc. The opposite happens, and she is the "*guilty*" of the death. Therefore, it has nothing to do with the physical death of the deceased, its function, its macabre task, is simply administrative. And since sometimes it does not succeed, because it arrives late and the person dies without receiving permission to enter "*the afterlife*", then they cannot stay in heaven, and that very humorously justifies the NDEs, which we talk so much about. these days, but in less humorous language.

Surely the reader has already realized, after reading - and perhaps enjoying - the previous humorous passage, that death, as a character, can mean the guarantee of obtaining a citizenship card when it comes to expanding the horizon of letters. In fact, in the world theater, death has played very interesting roles, and not only in the dramatic, as in that work of extraordinary beauty, which is "The Phantom of the Opera." (The Phantom of the Opera), film adaptation of the novel of the same name by Gastón Leroux, released in 2004.

It goes without saying that it does not mean that no author previously mixed the hereafter with the hereafter... To begin with, we have been doing it for years, only "illegally." But many works have been based in one way or another, placing characters in the afterlife, as cinema has done so many times with brilliant performance, only the reader-viewer accepts the context as part of the comedy, because otherwise I would turn off the TV or throw away the book.

Now the interesting novel "Doña Flor y sus dos Husbands" comes to mind (I feel like all of this is being suggested to me by the Dead Poets Club) by Brazilian **Jorge Amado**, made into a film by director **Bruno Barreto**, in 1978. Simply in cinema, above all, numerous works have been produced based on the unfolding of the being, with results that are generally very well handled and better received by viewers, because they are good comedies.

We can well list some works in which the theme of reincarnation, among others, has been used in literature.

3.1.1 Death does not know how to kill

Some authors who have used this context are:

- **Raymond Moody**: Philosopher and psychiatrist who published the book "*Life After Life*" in 1975, considered the pioneer in the study of NDEs. This book collects testimonies from people who lived experiences of light, tunnel, encounter with deceased loved ones, review of life and feeling of peace. etc Moody has also researched past life regressions and thinks, due to a hypnotic session conducted by psychologist Diana Denholm,[1] that he himself has had nine past lives. Moody also wrote poems inspired by NDEs, such as "*The Song of the Soul*" or "*The Return.*"

- **Elisabeth Kübler-Ross**: Psychiatrist and expert in thanatology who dedicated herself to supporting the dying and studying NDEs. He published the book "*Death: A Dawn*" in 2011, where he offers scientific proof of the existence of an afterlife. He also wrote poems about death and life after death, such as "*The Butterfly*" or "The Last Journey."

In Kubler, butterflies are a symbol of constant transformation thanks to their process of metamorphosis, that is, the passage from egg to caterpillar, from caterpillar to chrysalis and, finally, from chrysalis to butterfly. Therefore, butterflies are synonymous with perseverance and resilience, since they go a long way to reach their goal.

- Pim van Lommel: Dutch cardiologist who researched NDEs for twenty years and published the book "*Consciousness beyond life*" in 2012, where he offers abundant evidence that NDEs are a real phenomenon and not a hallucination. This author conducted case studies with patients who had suffered cardiac arrest. Based on his experience, he proposes that consciousness is not linked to the brain and that it can continue after death. Furthermore, he explains that NDE can have a profound impact on the lives of the people who experience them, changing their way of seeing the world and their values. He also wrote poems about NDE, such as "*The Awakening*" or "*The Light Within*."

- **James Merrill**. This Pulitzer Prize-winning American poet wrote an extensive poetic work influenced by his experiences of channeling and mediumship. Together with her partner, David Jackson, Merrill communicated with spirits through a "**ouija**" board, and expressed their messages in poems such as The Changing Books (1976) or The Quicksands (1982). Merrill considered poetry to be a means to access other dimensions of reality and other forms of knowledge.

- **José Hierro**. This Spanish poet, member of the Generation of '50 and Cervantes Prize winner, wrote several poems related to NDEs and the afterlife. In his book Cuaderno de Nueva York (1998), Hierro narrates his experience of being clinically dead for a few minutes after suffering a heart attack, and how that experience changed his perception of life and death. Hierro also reflects on reincarnation, channeling and mediumunity in other poems such as "*The Voice of the Other*" or "*The Fallen Angel*.".

Among the poets who have written about death and its mysteries, we can mention some such as **Mario Benedetti**, **Rainer María Rilke**, **Jorge Luis Borges, Alejandra Pizarnik** or **Nicomedes Santa Cruz**. These authors have expressed different views on the subject in their verses, from remorse to challenge, from sadness to hope. Some of his famous poems are: "*More or less death*", "*Death*", "*Remorse for any death*", "*Ballad on the crying stone*" and "*Death, if there were another death*", among others.

****

3.1.2 Death in poetry seen from a perspective of hope.

Investigating such a specific aspect could take years, and since it is not possible to do it in depth in a work of limited pretensions, we have used a search engine capable of locating specialized information, under the title that bears this heading, and we have obtained as answer the following, specifically using Bot Claude, which has limited its delivery to one example for each case considered. It is possible to expand the search, but we think that as an example of what the reader can also achieve on their own, it is enough.

- **Neruda**. It presents death as a new beginning to find love again.

  Neruda, P. (1974). Sonnet LXVI. In One Hundred Sonnets of Love (p. 145). Losada Editorial.

- **Borges. It raises the possibility of being born again as a form of** redemption after death.

  Borges, J.L. (1969). Remorse for any death. In The Other, the Same (p. 161). Emecé Editors.

- **Vallejo**. It suggests that after death there will be an awakening or resurrection to a new life.

  Vallejo, C. (1918). Spergesia. In The Black Heralds (p. 75). Peru Editions.

- **Agustini.** It proposes reincarnation into other forms of life after death like a swan.

  Agustini, D. (1910). The Cisne. In Complete Poems (p. 88). Claudio García Editor.

- **Peace**. It presents the continuity of consciousness after the dissolution of the physical body.

- **Paz,** O. (1957). Sunstone. In Parole (p. 77). Fund of Economic Culture.---

  ----

From a spiritual perspective, some criteria to analyze how the following poets approach the topic of death and reincarnation in their works:

- **Walt Whitman** in "Song of Myself": Presents death as a liberation of the soul to merge into the cosmos. It conveys a pantheistic vision.

  Whitman, W. (1855). Song of Myself. In Leaves of Grass. Fowler & Wells

- **Hermann Hesse** in "Stufen": It associates death with the concept of spiritual rebirth. It outlines the progress of the soul through successive lives.

  Hesse, H. (1905). Stufen. En Wanderung. Insel-Verlag

- **Octavio Paz** in "Hymn among ruins": Sees physical destruction as necessary for the renewal of the spirit. Suggests the eternal cycle of life, death and resurrection.

  Paz, O. (1957). Himno entre ruinas. En Libertad bajo palabra. Fondo de Cultura Económica

- **Rabindranath Tagore** in "Liberation": Describes death as the moment of encounter of the individual soul with the universal soul. Postulates transcendental unity.

  Tagore, R. (1913). Liberation. En Gitanjali. The India Society

- **Sor Juana Inés de la Cruz** in "First Dream": Presents the dream as a temporary prefiguration of life after death. Alludes to immortality.

  Sor Juana Inés de la Cruz. (1692). Primero Sueño. En Inundación Castálida. Imprenta de Bernardo Calderón.

- **William Blake** in "Omens of Innocence": It presents the cycle of reincarnation of the soul in animal and human form. Aims for spiritual perfectibility.

  Blake, W. (1789). Auguries of Innocence. En Songs of Innocence and of Experience. J. Johnson & J. Thomson.

With these references in APA format you can find the full texts of the original poems that were mentioned above when analyzing how they represent death and reincarnation from a spiritual point of view..

As you can see, several renowned poets have been able to integrate hope, continuity and rebirth as part of the death process. Conceptions that go beyond a limited vision of human existence.

From this perspective, death is not an absolute end but rather a transition towards a higher, fuller and liberated consciousness or existence. Poets manage to transmit these ideas with great sensitivity.

3.1.3 Poetic approach from authorship.

Many doubts have arisen for the author regarding the best way to conclude this work. In its genesis, following the pattern of the preceding work, "Hallucinations", the project was to begin with a chapter or introductory part, which would occupy the "theoretical" part – if these contents can already be called that – as a summary of the ECM context, so that the book as such would constitute the selection of poems that have been created, for the most part, with direct or indirect links, inspired by the NDEs, and written in the current year 2023. I have not been curious counting them, but the number may be greater than 50 poems, all published in at least two important sites: www.mundopoesía.com and www.poemas-del-alma.com In both sites the author has received interesting comments, which Thank you very much to the readers who have dedicated part of their time to give their sincere opinions.

But it happens that the space that has finally been required, to at least get closer to the vision that we wish to give in relation to the contents treated in the work, makes us rethink the initial idea, and choose to reduce the second part, that is, the collection of poems about ECM, limiting it to a selection that considers approximately a maximum of 20 poems, leaving the rest to then form a second volume of "**Hallucinations**", which would obviously include other themes, because a poetic work focused only on ECM poems, even if they were all of love, it would not be an easy read, if it finds readers capable of reading more than 80 poems related in some way to the image of death. But that would be another work, it is not there.

On the other hand, an acceptable selection of poems, combined with others to create a balance, which also include some criteria of comments made by readers, could be an appropriate complement to this work. From this perspective, which we hope will be attractive to readers, we enter the final curve of this effort, which in no way concludes the aspects discussed.

Simply, if in some way the work contributes to readers knowing a little more and becoming interested in or seeing the phenomena of the mind with a vision without limits, and above all that this allows them to better understand those works of any genre that arise inspired by the secrets that make us what we are as human beings, the many hours invested in its conception - let's forget about Quantum Mechanics for the moment - will not have been wasted time.

We finally clarify that, for the reasons explained in the introduction, the English version does not include the collections of poems from the original version, we only include a few poems, which come mostly from the work "**Mirage or reality**", presented without success to the contest **FRANCISCO BRINES 2023.**

3.1.4 Selection of commented poems

The final pages include a small selection of the author's poems, in which there is a presence of death, but assuming a very different position from the classic role.

1- MIRAGE OR REALITY

I see you and you disappear,
I look for you and you are no longer there.
I don't know if you exist or not,
In my surroundings I only find loneliness.
If I come into your life
I see you in all the mirrors,
but in none is your truth.
If we are together, I don't feel you,
your presence is absence,
but your absence is total presence:
I see you in all the mirrors
and your shadow shows that you exist,
but you can't touch it.

What are you then, if you are and you are not?

You are the mirage of my life,

you exist only in my sad unreality,

surreal drop that sometimes feeds me,

and at times, deadly poison...

Yes, you are always there, in every mirror of my life

like a paranoid image that you arrive and leave,

always present even in the most distant memories,

that are like mirrors of the past,

where only what exists is no longer there.

(1º/ abril/ 2023)

2- FROM FICTION - ECM-I

(Near Death Experience)

I look at you through my dreams

I only see your image that cries.

I would like to touch you and I can't,

and I don't want to leave you so alone.

They separate us and I can't understand it,

nor why have I slept with clothes,

I only know that I touch you and you don't feel,

and I don't agree to leave you so alone.

Confused, I can't tell you

I don't know why I see people,

They tell me that I have to go

and for nothing I leave you so alone.

I have finally convinced them,

and they tell me to continue my work,

I know nothing of what has happened,

but I know you won't be alone.

(19/ julio/2022)

3- REINCARNATION

I want to be in your life from beginning to end
to live on Earth once again,
the passion that two souls can only live,
when they are people,
when they are matter full of neurons...
Let us begin once again our journey to life,
Let's go back to that wonderful world
where two souls truly adore each other.
But look for me,
I will be waiting for you as always.
Only you have the key;
only you know the moment, the place and the time.

(7/ ene/ 2023)

4- LOVE IN THE TIMES OF QUANTUM PHYSICS

I have always trusted Science
thinking it is what it is.
And suddenly everything spins
and the world appears upside down.
It happens that what was was not,
and what was, never was.
I, simple mortal, who only know what I know,
I don't understand Bohr, nor Einstein,
and much less Bell...
Today I don't know if I exist or I don't exist.
I don't know if I ever loved...
It turns out that distances no longer exist
and space is multiverse,
and I... what will I be?
I only know that now you are asleep next to me;
and I can't believe that you are or are not...
In any case, I want to believe Grinberg's magic.
and accept that our brains are connected

and you listen between dreams what I think now,

even if you disappear later...

Love ,

listen to my thoughts,

intertwined forever

like Bell's electrons,

even if it's just a dream,

although Einstein didn't want to believe it.

Right now I don't know if you really are or not,

but at least for the last time,

hold my hands tight,

I do not want to lose you...

(3/ feb/ 2023)

5- IN SEARCH OF ETERNAL LOVE, A LETEO FOR TWO

I want you close, very close

God was not closer.

It doesn't matter if it's in Glory,

or in Lethe, both.

Since forgotten times,

great poets who have been,

They have cleaned up their forgetfulness,

in the sacred Lethe.

Together let's cross its waters,

to delete the above;

we will clean our minds,

without forgetting our love.

It is a path taken

in each reincarnation.

I want you close, very close

when we cross the two.

(18/ abril/ 2023)

6- PLANETARY SURREALISM

I feel overwhelmed by the weight of life,
and it is not due to the weight of the years.
Maybe I have lived in a time that is not mine,
or I was born on the wrong planet.
Seen this way,
I imagine living the surrealism of a life
that lasts millennia,
on an exoplanet where days last centuries,
and normal sex between humans lasts years...
A world where love for everything is intuitive,
and natural death does not exist, because we are eternal,
and accidents are mistakes of the past.
But let's be realistic...
A world like this would be very boring for many:
the early mornings would last more than a century,
and dreams, a lot of years.
Of course, there would be no crime,
because the sentences would be perpetual,
after an unbearable judicial process.
If you decide to go to the cinema or the theater, it would be a martyrdom,
and read this poem, don't even think about it…

(19/ abril/ 2023)

F I N

Original version of the poems - in Spanish

1-ESPEJISMO O REALIDAD

Te veo y desapareces,

Te busco y ya no estás.

No sé si existes o no existes,

en mi entorno solo encuentro soledad.

Si entro en tu vida

te veo en todos los espejos,

pero en ninguno está tu verdad.

Si estamos juntos, no te siento,

tu presencia es ausencia,

pero tu ausencia es presencia total:

te veo en todos los espejos

y tu sombra demuestra que existes,

pero no se puede tocar.

¿Qué eres entonces, si estás y no estás?

Eres el espejismo de mi vida,

existes solo en mi triste irrealidad,

gota surrealista que a veces me alimenta,

y por momentos, veneno mortal…

Sí, estas siempre allí, en cada espejo de mi vida

como imagen paranoica que llegas y te vas,

siempre presente hasta en los recuerdos más lejanos,

que son como espejos del pasado,

donde solo existe lo que ya no está.

(1º/ abril/ 2023)

2- DESDE LA FICCIÓN - ECM-I

(Experiencia Cercana a la Muerte)

Te miro a través de mis sueños

solo veo tu imagen que llora.

Quisiera tocarte y no puedo,

y no quiero dejarte tan sola.

Nos separan y no puedo entenderlo,
ni por qué he dormido con ropas,
solo sé que te toco y no sientes,
y no acepto dejarte tan sola.

Confundido no atino a decirte
que no sé por qué veo personas,
que me dicen que tengo que irme
y por nada te dejo tan sola.

Finalmente los he convencido,
y me dicen que siga mi obra,
Nada sé de lo que ha sucedido,
pero sé que no vas a estar sola.

(19/ julio/2022)

3- REENCARNACIÓN

Quiero estar en tu vida de principio a fin
para vivir en la Tierra, una vez más,
la pasión que dos almas solo pueden vivir,
cuando son personas,
cuando son materia llena de neuronas…
Comencemos una vez más nuestro viaje a la vida,
Regresemos a ese mundo maravilloso
donde dos almas se adoran de verdad.
Pero búscame,
yo estaré esperándote como siempre.
Solo tú tienes la clave;
solo tú sabes el momento, el lugar y la hora.

(7/ ene/ 2023)

4- EL AMOR EN LOS TIEMPOS DE LA FÍSICA CUÁNTICA

Siempre he confiado en la Ciencia
pensando que es lo que es.
Y de pronto toda da vueltas
y el mundo aparece al revés.
Sucede que lo que era no era,
y lo que fue, nunca fue.

Yo, simple mortal, que solo sé lo que sé,
no entiendo a Bohr, ni a Einstein,
y mucho menos a Bell...
Hoy no sé si existo o no existo.
No sé si amé alguna vez...
Resulta que las distancias ya no existen
y el espacio es multiverso,
y yo... ¿qué seré?

Solo sé que ahora estás dormida a mi lado;
y no puedo creer que estés o no estés...
En todo caso, quiero creer la magia de Grinberg.
y aceptar que nuestros cerebros están conectados
y escuchas entre sueños lo que ahora pienso,
aunque desaparezcas después...

Amor ,
escucha mis pensamientos,
entrelazados para siempre
como los electrones de Bell,
aunque solo sea un sueño,
aunque Einstein no lo quisiera creer.
Ahora mismo no sé si realmente eres o no eres,
pero al menos por última vez,
agárrame fuerte las manos,
que no te quiero perder...

(3/ feb/ 2023)

5- EN BUSCA DEL AMOR ETERNO, UN LETEO PARA DOS

Te quiero cerca, bien cerca
más cerca no estuvo Dios.
No importa si es en la Gloria,
o en el Leteo, los dos.

Desde tiempos olvidados,
grandes poetas que han sido,
han limpiado sus olvidos,
en el Leteo sagrado.

Juntos crucemos sus aguas,
para borrar lo anterior;
limpiaremos nuestras mentes,
sin olvidar nuestro amor.

Es camino recorrido
en cada reencarnación.
Te quiero cerca, bien cerca
cuando crucemos los dos.

(18/ abril/ 2023)

6- SURREALISMO PLANETARIO

Me siento agobiado por el peso de la vida,
y no es debido al peso de los años.
Quizás he vivido en un tiempo que no es el mío,
o nací en el planeta equivocado.

Visto así,
me imagino viviendo el surrealismo de una vida
que dura milenios,
en un exoplaneta donde los días duran siglos,
y el sexo normal entre humanos dura años...
Un mundo donde el amor a todo es intuitivo,
y la muerte natural no existe, porque somos eternos,
y los accidentes son errores del pasado.

Pero seamos realistas…
Un mundo así sería para muchos muy aburrido:
las madrugadas durarían más de un siglo,
y los sueños, un montón de años.
Claro, no habría delincuencia,
porque las condenas serían perpetuas,
después de un proceso judicial insoportable.
Si decides Ir al cine o al teatro, sería un martirio,
y leerse este poema, ni pensarlo…

(19/ abril/ 2023) -

F I N

REFERENCIAS

1) **Acosta, F, Pérez, Mª y Rodríguez, M**. (2022) ¿Sabes realmente qué es un paradigma? Una mirada a la Epistemología de Kuhn en tiempos post Kuhn. Editorial Académica Española. República de Moldavia.

2) **Arcangelis, N.** (2017). Manual práctico del medium. Editorial Sirio.

3) **Benítez, J.J.** (2023) El diario de Eliseo. Editorial Planeta

4) **Blake, W.** (1789). Auguries of Innocence. En Songs of Innocence and of Experience. J. Johnson & J. Thomson.

5) **Burton, R. (2012).** Does Cell Memory Explain Transplant Recipients Acquiring Donor's Traits? https://www.huffpost.com/entry/organ-transplant-cell-memory_n_1965477

6) **Cadavid, A**. (2004). Teoría Global del Universo Spaxium. EUROAMERICANA EDITORES. Descargado: 2/04/2017. http://myslide.es/documents/teoria-global-del-universo-spaxium.html

7) **Cannon, D**. (2010). Quantum Healing Hypnosis Technique: A Practical Guide and Handbook. Ozark Mountain Publishing, Inc.

8) **Carter, C**. (2010). Science and the afterlife experience: Evidence for the immortality of consciousness. Inner Traditions/Bear & Co.

9) **Carter, C. (2021).** Cellular memory in organ transplants. ScienceDaily. www.sciencedaily.com/releases/2021/04/210414095736.htm

10) **Cunningham, B**. (2009). A beginner's guide to hypnosis. The Journal of Innovative Psychotherapy, 1(1), 23-30.

11) **Doyle, A. C**. (2018). La historia del espiritismo. Editorial Humanitas.

12) **González, A**. (2019). La perspectiva de la muerte según diferentes culturas del mundo. Recuperado el 14 de julio de 2023, de [https://www.lavanguardia.com/cribeo/cultura/20191031/471329881768/perspectiva-muerte-diferentes-culturas-mundo.html]

13) **Goswami, A** (2012). Ciencia y espiritualidad. Una integración cuántica. Editorial Kairós, S. A.

14) **Greyson, B**. (2014). Near-death experiences and spirituality. Zygon, 49(2), 393-414. https://doi.org/10.1111/zygo.12086

15) **Hesse, H.** (1905). Stufen. En Wanderung. Insel-Verlag

16) **Joaniquet, V**., (s/f). ¿En qué nos puede ayudar las Canalizaciones espirituales? https://www.enbuenasmanos.com/canalizaciones-espirituales.

17) **Jose Luis García-Giménez** (2012). Journal of Feelsynapsis.JoF. ISSN 2254-3651. Número 4. Páginas 34-38.

18) **Kardec, A**. (1861). El libro de los médiums. París, Francia: Librairie des Sciences Psychologiques.

19) **Kardec, A**. (1864). El evangelio según el espiritismo. París, Francia: Union Spirite Française et Francophone.

20) **Kardec, A**. (1996). El libro de los médiums (Traducción revisada por S. Gentile). Instituto de Difusão Espírita. Mensaje Fraternal.

21) **Kardec, A**. (2019). El libro de los médiums (M. Arribas, Trans.; 12th ed.). Editorial Kier. (Trabajo original publicado en 1861).

22) **Kloppenburg, B**. (1993). La reencarnación. Editorial San Pablo. Bogotá.

23) **Kuhn, T**. (1971). La estructura de las revoluciones científicas.Trad. de A Cortin, Méxlco: FCE, 1971México.

24) **Lanza, R**. (2023). El gran diseño biocéntrico. Editorial Sirio.

25) **Lipton, B.,** (2005). The biology of belief: unleashing the power of consciousness, matter & miracles / Bruce H. Lipton, Ph.D. -- 10th anniversary edition. HAY HOUSE, INC. SBN: 978-1-4019-4891-7

26) **Lipton, Bruce H**. (2007) La biología de la creencia: la liberación del poder de la conciencia, la materia y los milagros. La Esfera de los Libros, 2007. ISBN 978-84-96665-18-7 https://www.brucelipton.com/es/

27) **Moody, R. A**. (1975). Life After Life: The Investigation of a Phenomenon-- Survival of Bodily Death. Mockingbird Books.

28) **Newton, M**. (1994). Journey of Souls: Case Studies of Life Between Lives. Llewellyn Publications.

29) **Newton, M**. (2000). Destiny of Souls: New Case Studies of Life Between Lives. Llewellyn Publications.

30) **Páez, Andrés** (2008). Explicaciones Científicas y No Científicas: El Problema de la Demarcación. En Juan José Botero, Álvaro Corral, Carlos Cardona & Douglas Niño (eds.), Memorias del Primer Congreso Colombiano de Filosofía. Volumen II. Universidad Jorge Tadeo Lozano. pp. 269-282.

https://philpapers.org/rec/PEZECY-2. Consultado: 19/ 02/ 2022)

31) **Pagels, Heinz R.** (1990). El código del universo: un lenguaje de la naturaleza, del físico. Traducción: Emilio Ibáñez de la Fuente y Marta Oyonarte Cálvez EDICIONES PIRÁMIDE, S. A., 1990

32) **Paz, O.** (1957). Himno entre ruinas. En Libertad bajo palabra. Fondo de Cultura Económica

33) **Pearsall, P. (1999).** The Heart's Code: Tapping the wisdom and power of our heart energy. Broadway Books.

34) **Pérez, M.** (2015). La muerte en la cultura occidental: antropología de la muerte. Revista Cubana de Salud Pública, 41(4), 681-691. Recuperado el 14 de julio de 2023, de [http://scielo.sld.cu/scielo.php?script=sci_arttext

35) **PsicoActiva.** (s.f.) El concepto de muerte en las diferentes culturas y religiones. Recuperado: el 14 de julio de 2023, de [https://www.psicoactiva.com/blog/el-concepto-de-muerte-en-las-diferentes-culturas-y-religiones/]

36) **Real Academia** de las Ciencias de Suecia. (2022). The Nobel Prize in Physics 2022. NobelPrize.org. https://www.nobelprize.org/prizes/physics/2022/summary/

37) **Sanchez Montalban, A.** (s/f). Qué es la canalización spiritual. Recuperado el 17 de julio del 2023. Ver: https://www.aprenderacanalizar.com/que-es-la-canalizaci%C3%B3n-espiritual

38) **Schwartz, R.** (2012). El plan de tu alma. Sirio Editorial.

39) **Sharp, J. (2021).** Organ Transplant Recipients Don't Acquire Memories from Their Donors. Scientific American. **https://www.scientificamerican.com/article/organ-transplant-recipients-dont-acquire-memories-from-their-donors/**

40) **Sor Juana Inés de la Cruz.** (1692). Primero Sueño. En Inundación Castálida. Imprenta de Bernardo Calderón.

41) **Tagore, R.** (1913). Liberation. En Gitanjali. The India Society

42) **Tighe, V. & Bernstein, L.** (1956). The Search for Bridey Murphy. Doubleday.

43) **Weiss, B. L.** (1988). Many Lives, Many Masters: The True Story of a Prominent Psychiatrist, His Young Patient and the Past-Life Therapy That Changed Both Their Lives. Simon & Schuster.

44) **Whitman, W.** (1855). Song of Myself. En Leaves of Grass. Fowler & Wells

45) **Wright, L.** (2022). Past life regression therapy: A systematic review and meta-analysis of its benefits. International Journal of Clinical Hypnosis, 64(3), 196-211.

46) **Xavier, F. C.** (2002). Evolución en dos mundos (8a ed.). Instituto de Difusão Espírita,

Páginas Web consultadas.

- Espiritismo - Wikipedia, la enciclopedia libre. https://es.wikipedia.org/wiki/Espiritismo.

- El Espiritismo – El progreso espiritual y la vida después de ....
  https://iluminando.org/2015/11/18/el-espiritismo-8-de-14-el-progreso-espiritual-y-la-vida-despues-de-la-muerte/.

- Espiritismo - Concepto, origen, historia, creencias y tipos.
  https://concepto.de/espiritismo/.

- Espiritismo x Espiritualidad: Principales diferencias en la visión de ....
  https://conteudoespirita.com/es/espiritismo-x-espiritualidad/.

- La perspectiva de la muerte según diferentes culturas del mundo.
  https://www.larazon.es/viajes/20200410/wckjpe2eubgvvmbydjrdoilpzm.html.

- El concepto de muerte en las diferentes culturas y religiones - PsicoActiva.
  https://www.psicoactiva.com/blog/concepto-muerte-las-diferentes-culturas-religiones/.

- La muerte en la cultura occidental: antropología de la muerte - SciELO.
  http://www.scielo.org.co/scielo.php?script=sci_arttextQué significa canalizar, mediumnidad e intuición - Spiral Aurea. https://spiralaurea.com/blog-evolutivo-espiritual/que-significa-canalizar-mediumnidad-e-intuicion/

- Xavier C.J, (15 6 1.997) .La Transcomunicación Instrumental. Descargado de:
  https://docplayer.es/16065638-La-transcomunicacion-instrumental-15-6-1-997.html

- ¿Qué explicaba la Teoría Sintérgica de Jacobo Grinberg? https://culturacolectiva.com/historia/que-explicaba-la-teoria-sintergica-de-jacobo-grinberg/

- La Teoría Sintérgica de Jacobo Grinberg Zylberbaum: experiencia, consciencia y unidad https://reflexionesmarginales.com/blog/2022/01/26/la-teoria-sintergica-de-jacobo-grinberg-zylberbaum-experiencia-consciencia-y-unidad/

- Jacobo Grinberg – Wikipedia https://es.wikipedia.org/wiki/Jacobo_Grinberg

- Grinberg, J. EL POTENCIAL TRANSFERIDO http://yosomos.wordpress.com/2010/03/08/segunda-parte-del-potencial-transferido/

- Experiencia cercana a la muerte - Wikipedia, la enciclopedia libre. https://es.wikipedia.org/wiki/Experiencia_cercana_a_la_muerte.

- Los mejores libros sobre Experiencias Cercanas a la Muerte. https://madrid.iacworld.org/experiencias-cercanas-a-la-muerte-libros/.

- 9 Poemas célebres sobre la muerte para reflexionar. https://versoslibres.com/poemas/9-poemas-sobre-la-muerte/.

- Las 7 experiencias de quienes "vuelven de la muerte" - BBC. https://www.bbc.com/mundo/noticias/2015/04/150326_vert_fut_cerca_muerte_lp.

- Esto es lo que se siente antes de morir según cinco testimonios con .... https://www.lavanguardia.com/cribeo/estilo-de-vida/20230212/8722976/esto-siente-morir-cinco-testimonios-experiencias-cercanas-muerte-mmn.html.

Debate científico:

- Novella, S. (2007). The Biology of Belief: A Pseudoscientific Theory. Neurologica Blog. https://theness.com/neurologicablog/the-biology-of-belief-a-pseudoscientific-theory/

Complejidad de la genética:

- Massey, D. S. (2016). A Critical Review of Lipton's The Biology of Belief. SPLASH! milk science update. https://milksci.unipi.it/wp-content/uploads/2016/04/massey-2016-critical-review-lipton-biology-of-belief.pdf

Interpretación simplista:

- Flamm, B. (2007). The Columbia University "Miracle" Study: Flawed and Fraud. Skeptical Inquirer. https://skepticalinquirer.org/2007/09/the-columbia-university-miracle-study-flawed-and-fraud/

Falta de evidencia empírica sólida:

- Dresser, N. (2007). The Biology of Belief: Unleashing the Power of Consciousness, Matter, & Miracles. Skeptic Magazine. https://www.skeptic.com/reading_room/the-biology-of-belief/

Posible sesgo y pseudociencia:

Offit, P. (2008). Biological Belief Systems. The New Republic. https://newrepublic.com/article/64634/biological-belief-systems

----

I want morebooks!

Buy your books fast and straightforward online - at one of world's fastest growing online book stores! Environmentally sound due to Print-on-Demand technologies.

Buy your books online at
www.morebooks.shop

Kaufen Sie Ihre Bücher schnell und unkompliziert online – auf einer der am schnellsten wachsenden Buchhandelsplattformen weltweit! Dank Print-On-Demand umwelt- und ressourcenschonend produziert.

Bücher schneller online kaufen
www.morebooks.shop

info@omniscriptum.com
www.omniscriptum.com

FSC
www.fsc.org

MIX
Papier aus verantwortungsvollen Quellen
Paper from responsible sources
FSC® C105338

Printed by Books on Demand GmbH, Norderstedt / Germany